Auritra Munshi

Jhumpa Lahiri's Works in Transition
Towards a New Space

With a foreword by Debjani Sengupta

Auritra Munshi

JHUMPA LAHIRI'S WORKS IN TRANSITION

Towards a New Space

With a foreword by Debjani Sengupta

ibidem
Verlag

Bibliographic information published by the Deutsche Nationalbibliothek
Die Deutsche Nationalbibliothek lists this publication in the Deutsche
Nationalbibliografie; detailed bibliographic data are available on the Internet at
http://dnb.d-nb.de.

Bibliografische Information der Deutschen Nationalbibliothek
Die Deutsche Nationalbibliothek verzeichnet diese Publikation in der Deutschen Nationalbibliografie;
detaillierte bibliografische Daten sind im Internet über http://dnb.d-nb.de abrufbar.

Cover picture: © copyright 2022 by Ritam Ghosal

ISBN-13: 978-3-8382-1758-1
© *ibidem*-Verlag, Hannover • Stuttgart 2024

Printed in the United States of America

Contents

Acknowledgements..7

Foreword 9

INTRODUCTION..13

Chapter 1:
Dialogues between multiple cultures: Reinterpreting diasporic
consciousness as loss and hope in *Interpreter of Maladies: Stories
of Bengal, Boston and Beyond* 33

Chapter 2:
Locational antipathy: A transnational mash up of emotion and
culture in *Unaccustomed Earth* 59

Chapter 3:
Diasporic Subjectivity: an aporetic journey in *The Namesake*.........81

Chapter 4:
Dialectic and differences: Towards a new cultural identity in
The Lowland 95

Chapter 5:
Celebration of *Italian Phase*: a new linguistic and cultural turn
in *In Other Words*..109

CONCLUSION 129

Bibliography...139

Index...145

Acknowledgements

Jhumpa Lahiri's works in Transition: Towards a new Space is basically borne out of my thesis. I have been dealing with Jhumpa Lahiri's works for a few years and more interestingly, have found a transition in her writings, which drives my attention to transmute my finding into a monograph. I am grateful to my PH.D supervisor, Prof. Pinaki Roy for his guidance and direction. Being my thesis adjudicators, Prof. Simi Malhotra and Prof. Amrit Sen praised my work a lot and suggested me to publish it in the form of a book; and their precious words were wide enough for my motivation to explore this area further. I am indebted to Prof. Himadri Lahiri for his support and encouragement that I am on the right track. I am beholden to Dr. Debjani Sengupta, who agreed to write a foreword for my monograph. I am also grateful to the Registrar of Raiganj University, Dr. Durlav Sarkar, for his institutional support. I must acknowledge the Deputy Librarian of Raiganj University, Mr. Ajay Misra, for his appropriate direction and support. My words will fail to convey my gratefulness to my better half, Surabhi, who always stood by me and encouraged me amidst the critical phase of her life. My parents (Baba, Maa) and my sisters and brother (Doll, Rim and Dibbo) were always with me as a support system. If my mother-in law were alive, she could have been elated with joy having watched the publication of my monograph. I am indebted to my esteemed colleagues for their support. I am immensely indebted to Ritam Ghosal, my friend, for the cover design of my book. Finally, I want to express my heartfelt thanks to the publishing house for accepting my proposal and thereby giving me an opportunity to refashion Jhumpa Lahiri in a new direction.

Foreword

I was born
With a forked
tongue.
Sabitha Satchi, Forked Tongue: A Preface

They were defined not by what they were — that was uncertain — but by what they
were not.
Siddhartha Deb, The Point of Return

Modern nationhood, globalization and mass communication make us all peculiar refugees: creating and unmaking ways of belonging and not belonging to a specific place or to the varied facets of our identities. This can be seen in the many diverse ways we live, or move away or choose to work in a specific locale. Global movements of people due to war or ecological disasters have added to the ways in which people have moved from place to place, subject to new order of things. In 1922, B. Traven's novel *The Death Ship* stated that 'the passport...and not the sun, is the center of the universe.' In this global era of mass migrations, Traven's words strike a fresh chord in our minds. As we approach a new era of interconnectedness yet polarizations, diametrically different from the earlier aspects of cosmopolitan travel and trade, liminality and transience mark the human subject just as the Romantic implications of the wandering diasporic subject is not lost too. To the writer who is born in one tongue and chooses to write in another, this movement is both internal and external: she chooses to inhabit a new language, both as a marker of her belonging and unbelonging: 'Diaspora can feel wrenching and liberatory by turns,' as Lawrence Buell states.

Multivocality in authors come to signify a new world order of simultaneously occupying multiple sites of belonging. The rising inequality across the world and perpetual political unrests in many parts of the globe have found new expressions and affects that challenge stereotypes of peoples and places: writers have come together to give voices to people who move and who challenge intellectual and aesthetic status quos. This imaginative

9

work, in particular, is carried out by authors who occupy different languages: choosing to write in one and then moving away into another. Jhumpa Lahiri, who is the focus of this present study, is such an author. Auritra Munshi takes up Lahiri's trajectory from a fiction to a non-fiction writer, then on to her journey as a translator, critically engaging with her parallel movements from a writer using English to Italian. In this journey, Munshi finds that this 'linguistic dislocation' allows the writer to find 'a new space in which she anticipates her freedom of choice, confronts difficulties,' and opens up possibilities of 'in between-ness,' and of a 'third space' both as a writer and as a postcolonial, transnational subject. Lahiri's earlier fiction, marked by alienation, homelessness, the uncertainty of a migrant in a new space, is now contextualized and refashioned with her own personal journey: she chooses to now read, write and translate from Italian. This study takes up a number of issues that are both pertinent and urgent in the global contexts of mass migration and neo-liberalism that I have touched upon right at the start. If modern diasporic imagination circumvents and subverts the nation state ideology then in what way does Lahiri's writings address the questions of cosmopolitanism, belonging and modernity? In her essay 'My Two Lives' Lahiri juxtaposes her growing up years as living in two worlds, 'falling short at both ends, shuttling between dimensions that had nothing to do with one another.' Living under the pressures of a bilingual and bicultural universe of her Bengali parents and Rhode Island school mates, Lahiri's fiction and non-fiction has moved between 'diasporic transmissions' that are organized around the unsaid and the unrepresentable. This study seeks to explore some of those gaps of transmission, the ambivalences and desires of living and speaking in forked tongues.

In many ways, Jhumpa Lahiri forges a path that had been marked in the earlier phases of literary modernity in her mother tongue Bangla. Notable writers of repute who wrote primarily in Bangla but were well versed in English or other European languages, moved easily between the many worlds of multivocality and translations: Buddhadev Bose comes most readily to mind. So were Alokeranjan Dasgupta, Nabaneeta Dev Sen, Amiyo Deb and others who were versatile poets and artists with a unique cosmopolitan imagination that did not seek to measure the world in binaries. The present study situates Jhumpa Lahiri not only within a diasporic imaginative world but also explores her oeuvre that creates new paradigms for conceptualizing the self's relation to others, both in terms of space and history. As we live under the shadow of systematic racism, ultra-nationalism and forms of institutional oppression, the critic (and in turn those whose business is literary studies) must reformulate a 'critical routine' that would, in the words of Bruce Robbins, be constructing something rather than blasting away. The job of the critic is to interrogate and to put events of the present unto a meaningful relationship with the events of the past. On the other hand, literary transgressions, in form and content, are the hallmarks of a versatile writer who traverses many linguistic and geographical spaces and maps, in Arjun Appadurai's words, the 'scapes' of history, economy and culture. Munshi's study of Jhumpa Lahiri's literary output maps the interface between a critic's interrogation and a writer's transgressions in many distinct ways.

Dr. Debjani Sengupta
Associate Professor of English
Indraprastha College for women
Delhi University, India

INTRODUCTION

> The end of all our exploring
> Will be to arrive where we started,
> And know the place for the first time (49-59)
> — T.S. Eliot's "Little Giddings"

Critical discussion of Jhumpa Lahiri's fiction is rampant, but they are confined to her short stories and fictions. This book offers a fresh perspective by showing how she, while occupying a prestigious position in the gallery of Indian-American Writers, gradually shifts her identity from that of a fiction writer to a writer of non-fiction-a shift, which is rare in the literary field. There is a sudden change in her writing, her choice of language; she prefers Italian to English and Bengali. Such spatial as well as linguistic dislocation leads her towards a new space in which she anticipates her freedom of choice, confronts difficulties, and often gets confused too: to be in Italy or not to be. Such confusion is starkly represented in her non-fiction *In Other words* (2016). More interestingly, Italy, if one looks at it from the geographical vantage point, is situated roughly between India and America. It is indicative of, in-between-ness, possibilities of anticipating a 'third space'. In her essay "My Two Lives" (2006), Jhumpa Lahiri speaks earlier of the pressure which emanates from the two different cultural milieus: Bengali and English as she has to be loyal to the Bengali culture and fluent in the English, too. Of late, Lahiri feels a natural affinity towards Italy and Italian language in which she refers to the imposition of Bengali and English language on her; Italy now is her favourite space from where she starts her journey anew. Jhumpa Lahiri is a transnational figure, to be observed from her short story collection, *Interpreter of Maladies: Stories of Bengal, Boston, and Beyond* (1999) to her recently published work *Translating Myself and others* (2022). Being a diasporic writer, she remains a perpetual traveller, as her fictional characters are. She goes beyond the cartographical epistemology, and is against the conception of 'ghettoization'. Her fictional stories not only show the Bengali culture, but create a ground of cultural di(a)ssociationby celebrating different cultural values together. Her travelling narratives in the words of James Clifford, refer to a 'different mode of dwelling and displacement', 'different trajectories and identities' in the 'post-colonial world of global contacts'. Apart from her fiction, her non-fiction writings also refer to her translational and transnational existence.

Women diasporic writers with their sensibility, imagination and emotion germinate a different space in the realm of literature. Especially women writers from the Asian sub-continents become quite sound on account of their explicit manifestation to the world outside their homeland as well as their grounding and orientation in the cultural traditions of the homeland. Indian writings in English have matured to a great extent in abroad by the present 21st-century. However, if the history of the women writers is reviewed, it begins from the middle of the 19th century A.D. when Toru Dutt (1856-77) penned some extraordinary works in English at a very young age. Other names also follow in the list such as Swarnakumari Ghosal (1855-1932), Krupabai Satthianadhan (1862-94), Shevantibai Nikambe (1865-1930), Cornelia Sohrabji (1866-1954), Sarojini Naidu (1879-1949), and Rajlukshmee Debee Bhattacharya (1927-2005), who have carved a niche for themselves in the field of Indian fiction. Their works consist of relationships, society, identity, conflicts and patriotism. This tradition of writing further progressed by the women writers of this age. There are famous novelists like Nayantara Sahgal (b. 1927), Anita Desai (b. 1937), Shashi Deshpande (b. 1938), Manju Kapoor (b. 1948), Shobha De (b. 1948) and many other women writers who have success-fully delved into female heart and mind in a language that is read by most part of the world. Not only these women writers of India, but the women writers of Indian diaspora such as Anita Desai (b. 1937), Bharati Mukherjee (1940-2017), Chitra Banerjee Divakaruni (b. 1956), Anita Rau Badami (b. 1961), Jhumpa Lahiri (b. 1967), Ruchira Banerjee, and Anjali Banerjee and others with their femi-nine sensibility have unfurled the process of retaining their exist-ence in the realm of literary canon by dint of their imaginative faculty. Women, perceptively being more sensitive about personal relationships, the religion, customs and traditions, suffer more in the new homeland. Their stories are based on the loss of their cultural identities, sense of alienation, homelessness, the uncertainty of their life in the new surroundings and the complexity that arises due to the female psyche in the context of her own self and the west that is so foreign to them in terms of living, customs, rituals, dressing, attitude towards relationships and their total attitude towards life in general. Not only is the physical displacement due to immigration explored, but the psychological impact of this dislocation on the psyche of the women immigrants is also delineated and expressed vigorously yet delicately in their literary works.

'Diaspora' for humans, mentioned first with reference to the dispersal of Greeks in the Hellenic World, and later Jews after the Babylonian exile, involves scattering from one place to another which may lead to a sort of split personality or hyphenated identity, too. Hence, hyphens are intimidating agencies from which both Bharati Mukherjee and Jhumpa Lahiri have tried to extricate themselves. It is emblematic of their cosmopolitan stance. Bharati Mukherjee found her 'brave new land' in the United States of America after rejecting Canada whereas Lahiri seems to need a neutral ground—neither Indian nor American. Displacement of the diasporic individuals in the host country widens a space of generating their ethnic enclave or fellow feelings by remembering their past associated with their ancestral home culture. This cross-current of the local populace emanates from their home and the demand of the global stems from their host culture, creating a 'soft space' which makes the immigrants 'glocal'. However, the increasing tendency of migration from a South Asian country to the so-called 'first world', which is considered as brain drain, unsettles the contours of the geographical borders, and places the immigrant individuals in a state of translocation. This so-called 'cyber coolies', who migrate due to their free will, are considered as *masala diaspora* in accordance with Sudesh Mishra. Thus, they relive or reconstitute their entity with difference in the host country. In fact, the global capitalism has a great role to play in immigration act as well. These South Asian people, who postulate their existence in the host culture, are termed as a 'model minority'; it disrupts the propensity to go for the original location of the home which falls into the concept of *imagined communities* by Benedict Anderson. Avtar Brah describes 'diaspora' as "conceptual mapping which defies the search for originary absolutes, or genuine and authentic manifestation of a stable, pregiven, unchanging identity" (196). In her *Cartographies of Diaspora,* she makes a distinction between 'home' and 'Homing desire' (192). However, this homing-desire, which is prevalent within the diasporic individuals, tends to make one rhizomatic having no specific location. Homi K. Bhabha has discussed the feeling of 'unhomeliness' often mentioned by migrants. In *The Location of Culture* (1994), he writes that to be 'unhomed' does not mean to be homeless; yet it is difficult to accommodate the 'unhomely' in the familiar division between private and public spheres. In the process of displacement, in Bhabha's words, "the borders between home and world become confused; and, uncannily, the private and public become part of each other, forcing upon us a vision that is as divided as it is disorienting" (9). Home in the diaspora becomes a fictive concept which is constituted by means of imagination of the immigrants. This has made an impact on diasporic subjectivity which is both performative and nomadic. However, writing previously about the concept of home in diasporic writings, William Safran commented,

> Diasporic community includes several categories of individuals (refugees, expatriates, alien, residents, ethnic and racial minorities) living outside their homeland and sharing a series of common features, such as a history of dispersal, visions and memories of lost homeland, alienation in the host land, yearning for an eventual return and collective identity. (83)

Hence, modern diaspora circumvents, to borrow Clifford's term, the 'nation state ideology' (308) with regard to identity. Now, electro-communication and mass media constitutes "diasporic public sphere" (Appadurai 5) which refers "to the cultural dynamic of urban life in most countries and continents, in which migration and mass mediation constitute a new sense of the global as modern and the modern as global" (*ibid* 10). A kind of cosmopolitan aspect can be located within the modern diasporic people. As Arjun Appadurai states,

Electronic mass mediation and transnational mobilization have broken down the monopoly autonomous Nation-States over the project of modernisation. The transformation of everyday subjectivities through electronic mediation and the work of the imagination is not only a cultural fact. It is deeply connected to politics, through the new ways in which individual attachments, interests and aspirations increasingly crosscut those of the nation-state. (*ibid.* 10)

The immigrants' desire to follow the host culture and re-live by invoking their past memories of home- are emblematic of their constant oscillation between these two worlds, which consequently place them in the realm of contingency; it is bereft of a spacio-temporal barrier as well. So the constitution of the diasporic subject having its nomadic growth and potentiality relies on the process of differing that poses a question to the traditionalist, culturalist demand of a model community. Fanon describes it in *The Wretched of the Earth* as "the zone of occult instability where the people dwell" (182-83). This is what Deleuze describes as "a veritable theatre of metamorphoses and permutations" (56). This is a theatre a "world without identity" (*ibid.*57), where everyone is oscillating between the finitude of being in specific times and places, and the infinitude of being's becoming" (*ibid.*57), which indicates the space of the trans-nation. Jhumpa Lahiri's fictional characters represent such a space of trans-nation by means of their fluidity. In fact, the intermixture of cultures and races, and the cross-cultural dialogue gives rise to two structures, which Robert J. C. Young describes as "a structure of attraction, where people and culture intermix and merge, transforming themselves as a result, and a structure of repulsion, where the different elements remain distinct and are set against each other dialogically" (19). Emigrants cross the border for many reasons. They are caught in cultural crossroads in the host land, and consequently, it generates ambivalence as well as a different sort of space called 'Third Space'. However, immigrants create their space by means of their imagination:

Memory is the smooth space that flows through and around the striated space of history, the space of the nation state and all structures of fixed identity. Ironically, memory, through the medium of literature, becomes the vehicle of potentiality rather than stasis. (qtd .in Ashcroft 22)

Diasporic characters can live by recreating or practicing their own cultural tools within the host culture that generates their willingness to relive their culture, and they can be interested in the assimilationist principle to make a rapport with the mainstream culture: it evokes a hybridised world for them. The diasporic characters are to suffer from "double consciousness". On the one hand, they get interpellated into the host subject, and on the other, they are carried away by their own home culture. This to-and-fro movement makes them sandwiched. However, diasporic discourse assimilates together both roots and routes to construct what Gilroy describes as 'alternative public sphere' (237): a form of community consciousness and solidarity that retains identification outside the national time and space to live inside, with a difference. In fact, the term 'diaspora' is a signifier, not simply of transnationality and movement, but of defining the *glocal*. More importantly, Jhumpa Lahiri creates a cultural syncretism and hybridity or cultural osmosis. Tagore wrote,

> Nationalism is a great menace. It is the particular thing which for years has been at the bottom of India's troubles. And as much as we have been ruled and dominated by a nation that is strictly political in its attitude, we have tried to develop within ourselves, despite our inheritance from the past, a belief in our eventual political destiny. (47)

Tagore feels a dire necessity to sweep away this nationalistic fervour which genuinely hinders the progress of the Nation. However, Tagorian principle seems to have matched with Lahiri as she is not nationalistic in exploring her home culture like typical Indians or the coloured; rather, she takes recourse to blending the home and host, a stance that carries the whiff of cosmopolitanism. She tries to dismantle the boundaries between nations, seeming not to believe in Robert Frost's belief that "Good fences make good neighbours" (Robert Frost in "Mending Wall", line number 46) — rather she seeks to celebrate the hospitality of the host culture while having acquaintance with the home culture. Tagore indicates the need for unity, not uniformity. Similarly, Lahiri, by bringing her characters together, wants to do away with any sort of nationalistic fervour or uniformity; she rather wants to club cultures of various kinds together in an attempt to form a salad bowl denoting unity in diversity. Lahiri seems to have been inspired by the Derridean concept of 'Unconditional hospitality'. Hence, her approach is humanitarian. She deals with multiple cultures and languages which will prove her stature as a cosmopolitan writer. Cosmopolitan aspects which Jhumpa Lahiri seeks to unpack throughout her works appear to be resonating with Seyla Benhabib's concept of 'Another Cosmopolitanism'; it entails a kind of cosmopolitanism which will emerge from the linguistic and cultural iteration of people. Such cosmopolitanism is pertaining to the theme of people-driven hospitality which can be termed in view of Benhabib as 'democratic iteration'. According to Benhabib "Democratic iterations are linguistic, legal, cultural and political repetition in-transformation" (48). Such performativity of Lahiri and her fictional characters in the home and the host refer to her transitional attitude.

In one of the more sensitive mediations of the conditions of exile and its Manichean relationship with the nation, Edward Said has suggested that "the interplay between nationalism and exile is like Hegel's dialectic of servant and master, opposites informing and constituting each other" (50). Lahiri really tries to create a Utopic World by yielding importance to the imagination. In the absence of a predefined and prominent 'home', she drifts from one place to another, one culture to another, and, presently, she is absorbed in Italian Language. She is actually a cultural pilgrim having the potential to create her own world with a difference from the actual. The nation is actually a political metaphor which is generally forged out of culture, society and political aspects: these subtexts come together synergetically. The idea of a nation can be compared to the text whose existence is embedded in terms of performance. Under the rubric of the feminist ground, the nation is considered as a female figure by Sarah Milles. According to her, intrusion of the British (phallic intrusion) to the Nation appears to be "soft touch" (2), suggesting that "Nations borders are like soft skin, they are soft, weak, porous and easily shaped or bruised by the proximity of others" (*ibid.* 2). The use of the metaphors 'softness' and 'hardness' shows how emotions become attributes of collectives, which get constructed as 'being' through feelings. Such attributes are of course gendered. The "soft nation" body is "feminised body which is penetrated or invaded by others" (Ahmed 2). Those who have touched, bruised this soft nation body hold the position of the centre. However, in the postcolonial axis, the centre is somehow replaced by the margins or displaced persons, namely 'the colonised', 'women', 'the migrant', and 'the immigrant' who are prone to generate their canon by rewriting history; it is attuned to a sort of 'Second Coming': "things fall apart/centre cannot hold" (Yeats 3). The politicised history served by the centre seems to be a grand narrative; but in the postcolonial ground, migrants or displaced persons raise their voices to compose their periphery testifying to the celebration of fragments or micro-narratives. They attempt to decolonize the colonial presence projecting their dissident voices. Hence, the 'nation' invariably falls into the system of signs with its inherent instability which is validated by the act of performance that militates against the geographical barrier of the nation and valorises the concept of 'Imagined Communities' by Benedict Anderson. A nation is nothing but narration, and having its porosity and borders seems to be like 'mending wall' which is entrenched in—to use the Lacanian term—'suturing' (276). So, the Nation-State ideology stands on the flimsy ground in the postcolonial grid, which is furthermore accentuated by the dropping of the Midnight bomb by Salman Rushdie in the South Asian literary canon. In fact, Salman Rushdie, Amitav Ghosh, and some other diasporic writers seek to shadow the geographical contours constituting the nation, and plead for *chutnification* which connotes the ensconce of the diasporic cogito in a cultural plexus. It becomes overt while it is premised upon a transcultural encounter which leads us to Bill Ashcroft's notion of 'Presence' referring to an 'uncanny space', and it 'becomes, potentially, a space of negotiation' (76). It not only talks about cultural, linguistic alienation, but also ponders over the psychic alienation that refers to trauma. The continuous deferral of diasporic subjectivity or immigrants is interpellated into any specific hegemonic subject, such as home or host, global or local, which render mental disequilibrium to them, and thus leading one to be intimate with her own world which breaks down all sorts of fences. Lahiri's works have the potential to dismantle cultural, spatio-temporal, social and linguistic barriers.

Jhumpa Lahiri's narrative, to review, is steeped in the blending of fiction and autobiography filtered through a dual lens, even though she admitted that while growing up in Rhode Island in the 1970s, she felt neither Indian nor American. In her "My Two Lives", she proclaims,

> Like many immigrant offspring I felt intense pressure to be two things, loyal to the old World and fluent in the new, approved of on either side of the hyphen. Looking back, I see that this was generally the case. But my perception as a young girl was that I fell short at both ends, shuttling between two dimensions that had nothing to do with one another. (43)

Lahiri seeks to go in and out of the hyphen for boning up on both the sides. She differs from the writers like Bharati Mukherjee or Chitra Banerjee Divakaruni, with whom she is often paralleled, in that she is a second-generation non-resident Indian whose interest in her roots is like that of an intelligent and sensitive tourist. While the former admire American freedom and adopt traditional Indian cultural norms, she has the emancipatory potential to abandon the nascent imbroglio and trot out a neutral or balanced representation of the two cultures. She is, in fact, the first author of Indian origin living in the United States of America who received the *Pulitzer Prize for literature* in 1999. Prior to her, Gobinda Behari Lal (1889-1982) had also won the same award, but for reporting. Lahiri's acknowledgement as an author of American tradition(s) — and not merely as a South Asian writer — changes the unilateral dimension of looking at the ethnic writers from the mainstream or White writers' part. Indeed, Lahiri has nicely been placed with the White Writers array on account of her mobility in terms of her style. She becomes a very prominent writer in the U.S. literary canon which is indicative of the gradual alteration of mainstream culture's outlook towards "the ethnic groups and their cultural products, a change that has been taking place slowly ever since the Civil Rights Movements in the 1960s" (qtd. in Lahiri 131). It would, however, be naïve to assume that the White literary historians have given up their prejudice altogether about the 'ethnic' writers. Although the United States of America is usually referred to, internationally, as 'a nation of immigrants,' the general American attitude to 'non-traditional' immigrants has always been ambiguous at best, and racial at the worst. Lisa Lowe, in *Immigrant Acts: On Asian American Cultural Politics* (1996), analyses how the notion of citizenship was manipulated to exclude Asian immigrants. She argues that the early immigrants from the Asian countries had to "inhabit the political space of the [American] nation, a space that is, at once, juridically legislated, territorially situated, and culturally embodied" (3). The "administration of citizenship was simultaneously a 'technology' of racialization and gendering" (*ibid.* 11). The immigrants who contributed to the making of the nation were denied citizenship and their foundational contributions were sought to be erased. In his *The Forgetful Nation* (2005), Ali Behdad considers this erasure as a deliberate 'amnesia.' Citing the instance of Ellis Island Museum erasing the painful history of immigrants from non-privileged countries, he observes that "American national culture [...] has always embodied a nativist or anti-foreign component to manufacture an imagined sense of community" (10). It is "an amnesic nation that persistently disavows its violent beginnings to fashion an imagined democratic community" (*ibid.* 6). A process of filtering, he argues, operates to shut out "some knowledge" (*ibid.* 9). "To be an immigrant", he observes, "implies by definition a certain attachment to another country, an attachment consequently marked as 'un-American'" (*ibid.* 11). This mindset about the immigrants and children of the immigrants being attached elsewhere, and not to the United States of America, operated not only in the political sphere but also in the socio-cultural areas. "It is precisely because of the inclusion of Lahiri in the general American canon, and not just in the 'ethnic' canon, should be considered a landmark event" (qtd. in Lahiri 131).

Lahiri always feels distanced from putting herself in any particular cultural hegemony which seems to be impediment to her freedom being a creative artist. She herself proclaims,

As an author, I could embody any individual my imagination enabled me to, of any origin. This sense of freedom is one of the greatest thrills of writing fiction, and for a person like me, who has never been confident of what to call herself or of whether to say she is from, it is a solace. ("Intimate Alienation" 1)

Viewing the world through 'sensory organs' tends to possess the objective reality of the world; this is what the empiricist school believes. Whatever stems from this world through the human cognitive faculty is truth or knowledge which denotes passivity of mind as if the human individual is a passive recipient of the corporeal knowledge from this materialistic world (Locke, Hume, and Leibnitz are emblematic of the cognitive world or corporeality only) but Kant brings out the duality of every object which is sundered into two categories such as an empirical- 'things as it is' and a metaphysical or transcendental 'things in itself'. In order to go beyond the categorical imperatives, Kant refers to the imaginative faculty of the human individuals. Jhumpa Lahiri, a second-generation diasporic and creative writer, also cashes in on the imagination to transmute the objective reality, she observes India but the way she represents it is nothing but re-creating her world via her fictive language. She herself proclaims "I translate therefore I am" ("Intimate Alienation" 5), which reinforces her creative impulse by uprooting herself from any sort of cartographical epistemology. She has unravelled her own experience of the world through her fictions, and such fiction is being rendered different rubrics in different places. Her composition is basically treated as 'Diaspora fiction' in the Indian context and 'Immigrant fiction' in the American context. Moreover, she has been defined as an 'Anglo-Indian', an 'NRI', an 'ABCD' (*American born confused desi*) and a 'desi author' in different places referring to her 'nomadic' identity. She is reconciled to her alienation to celebrate her independence as a living being and creative writer in a country where she lives and simultaneously anticipates her interdependence by forming a bridge between home and host which acts as a mind/body duality intrinsic to each other. Although she believes that she belongs to nowhere and delimits any specific 'nation-state ideology', she admits: "I have always lived under the pressure to be bilingual, bicultural, at ease on either side of Lahiri family map" ("Intimate Alienation" 1). And she has gone through the socialisation at home via her Bengali language and culture. Her parents, first-generation immigrants, were bent on keeping their ancestral culture alive by means of performing their ethno-cultural slabs in the host country; it creates an ambivalent space for her. They have resorted to memory in order to re-generate their homeland within the host land. On the other hand, the members of the second-generation immigrants have, in Arjun Appadurai's phrase, 'nostalgia without memory' (30). The members of the American-born generation see the family as problematic space, a site for contestation of cultural values.

Lahiri has always suffered from word vis-à-vis world dichotomy as her linguistic world has been splintered in two. She says,

> I have always lived under the pressure to be bilingual, bicultural, at ease on other side of the Lahiri family map. The first words I learned to utter and understand were in my parents' native tongue Bengali. Until I was old enough to go to school, and my linguistic world split in two, I spoke Bengali exclusively and fluently. Though I still speak Bengali, I have lost this extreme fluency. I was stunned, listening a few years ago to a cassette tape that had recorded the wedding of one of my parents' friends, in 1970 cassette-tape that had recorded the wedding of one of my parents' friends in 1970. (Lahiri, "Intimate Alienation" 2)

Lahiri refers to this process of 'desi' (native) culture's 'being alive' within the 'videsi' (foreign) culture by resorting to technology like 'tape recorder'. There is a linguistic schism in Lahiri in terms of having pure knowledge regarding the Bengali language and her acquired language like English. English seems to be ponderous enough to subsume her inherent potential of clear understanding of Bengali language. She refers to the 'vacuum culture' (a term coined by Gauri Bhat, and quoted in Mishra 184), which finds its resonance in her fictional characters too. Belonging to both 'here' and 'their', U.S.-born children nonetheless face a tremendous impossibility of a permanent return. Owing to such vacuum upbringing, they are conscious of their ethnicity as they aim to process the hyphen. Jhumpa Lahiri's fictional characters in her prose seem to testify to the same so far as diasporic identity formation is concerned. Thus she occupies a prestigious position in the gallery of Indian-American writers. Writing, for Lahiri, is a means of being at home, of finding a home, as she articulates in an interview with Tom Vitale in 2008: "I never felt that I had any claim to any place in the World. But in my writing, I have found my home, really, in a very basic sense-in a way that I never had one growing up." Lahiri unfurls her stories through her narration, which is steeped in exploring not only diasporic anxieties rather intricacies of human relationships too. Her collection refers to a "decisive orientation towards anxieties of the diaspora in the place where they are at, not where they came from" (191). Thus, Lahiri is intent on exposing cultural translation, about first-generation Indian immigrants coming to cope with the anxieties stemming from alienation due to displacement and their struggle to master a new landscape, to map and read it as 'natives' do. Lahiri seeks to propose her 'amalgamated domain' (Lahiri, "Intimate Alienation" 4) by means of projecting hybridised language too. She writes,

> I think I would narrate the expository passages in English while preserving all the dialogue, where appropriate, in Bengali. Such tactics are not feasible for a general audience, except in very short doses. In some instances I do retain Bengali words in my stories. The *durwan* of 'A Real Durwan' is one example. I liked the sound of the word in Bengali, and the full phrase, with the two English words in front of it, sounded perfectly normal, just as it is normal for me and even for my parents to slip the occasional English word into Bengali conversation. (Even the coinage A.B.C.D. betrays a similar linguistic hybridization.) The phrase *bechareh*, an epithet used to designate a pitiable person, also appears in 'A Real Durwan'. I included it not out of any need to be culturally accurate, but due to the whims of my own quasi-bilingual brain. ("Intimate" 4)

This is how Lahiri retains her objectivity in representing any particular culture which confirms dialogic connection, multicultural aspects and plurality. Imbibing 'strategic essentialism' as a tool, she conforms to (alter)native identity, too. She performs ethnic culture and host cultural milieus also in an attempt to take a neutral position. Translation so becomes a very important part of her writing as she herself ejaculates, "Almost all of my characters are translators, insofar as they must sense of the foreign in order to survive." ("Intimate" 4). Harish Trivedi agrees that translation is a fitting metaphor which can be deployed to unveil the people belonging across nations and Cultures. He sets up an accurate connection between Lahiri's use of the verb 'survive' and Bhabha's concept of living on the borderlines, which becomes the migrant's dream of survival; an initiatory interstice; an empowering condition of hybridity" (qtd.in Trivedi 5). Lahiri states in her essay that unlike her parents, who are first generation immigrants, she no longer has to translate in order to survive in the new world, but does so in order "to create and illuminate a nonexistent one" ("Intimate" 5). As Floyd and Dhingra write, Lahiri in order to

> make sense of the 'foreign' almost always conjures thoughts of cultural, linguistic, and national displacement. But if we juxtapose the idea that Lahiri admits that all of my characters must make sense of the foreign in order to survive alongside the title of her collection and the title story itself, I argue that we have to consider that the foreign can be something beyond the linguistic and cultural. If we ponder the interpretation and translation of psychic maladies and not language nor culture, what do we find?. (119)

Psychic maladies are more often than not caused by loss or traumatic experience. Cathy Caruth thus writes of trauma:

> the event is not assimilated or experienced fully at the time, but only belatedly, in its repeated possession of the one who experiences it. To be traumatised is precisely to be possessed by an image or event. The traumatized, we might say, carry an impossible history within them, or they become themselves the symptom of a history that they cannot entirely possess. (ibid. 119)

Lahiri translates the foreign and the inassimilable nature of trauma and loss that wound each of the characters in her stories.

In a 2010-interview, "Lahiri expressed the peculiarities of her second-generation experience not in cultural terms but in terms of feeling, that of an 'abyss very choice'. This has encouraged me to think of diasporic transmissions — perhaps most transmissions — as that which is organized around the unsaid, the un-representable, the gap, the emptiness, all of which are framed by ambivalence and desire" (qtd. in Munos xiiii). In fact, being a second-generation immigrant, Lahiri hints at the 'symbolic incarceration' (Ibid xxvii) on the part of the first-generation immigrants, which leaves a negative impact on the second-generation and third-generation immigrants. It invariably leads them to a buffer zone, and thus makes their life acerbic. In-fact, People who consider themselves as a part of diaspora form an imaginary; it is a landscape of dream and fantasy that answers to their desires. This desire prompts one to be an alienated individual and thus helps one explore his or her heterogeneous identities. It yields to her fiction and non-fiction a hetero-cosmic nuance too. Diasporans in general and Lahiri in particular suffer from (dis)ease because being separated from the root and route, they can generate their own space replete with loss and gain too. It refers to their ease and disease also which entails the implicit connotation of translation. Rushdie says via translation one can gain something and lose something where as Lahiri proclaims, 'I translate therefore I am' ("Intimate" 5), which resonates individual potential or subjecthood entrenched in flickering motion. And by dint of performances, it continuously alters its position. Her recent engagement with the Italian language, and culture testifies to the same. It sounds like the Spivakian dictum, "Desire does not lack anything; it does not lack its object. It is, rather, the subject that is lacking desire, or desire lacks a fixed subject" (5), and therefore continuous performances of subjecthood in and across continents go through a dialectic process, leading towards a path which is entwined with desire, power, and thus subjectivity is in motion. In fact, alienation, a kind of process, can be of various types, such as social, economic, cultural, linguistic and psychological. The diasporic individuals are always bent on building up their own individual identity while they interact or encounter with others. But being in difficulty to negotiate with the social as well as familial space, they amputate themselves from the other self/selves to create their sole world of utopia. However, encountering a gap between the actual world in which they live and the utopian world in which they aspire to live, individuals' souls and minds become a stage of dialogues and a struggle between conflicting emotions and orientations. In fact, Lahiri's fluid ontology, experience of home and homelessness, and more importantly, her adherence to a different language, Italian, reinforce her alienation and drive her to establish her intimate space. It offers her freedom and artistic agency to blur the boundaries of any form, and thereby revealing her literary transition as well as transgression.

This book is divided into seven chapters along with an introduction and conclusion. In **the introduction**, the book will aim to show the theme of diaspora and transnationalism, and how they intersect at a point and deviate. Memory, alienation, cross-pollination of cultures and others have been dealt with in a nuanced way. The introductory chapter discusses the various diasporic thesis and locates Jhumpa Lahiri within the historiography of the literature of diaspora. It also emphasizes on, through the discussion of Jhumpa Lahiri's fictional and non-fictional writing, how Jhumpa Lahiri becomes a global soul by shifting her identity in terms of language, culture and society. Lahiri's recent adherence to the *Italian Phase* will help us track down the transition in her works.

In **the first chapter**, I have tried to analyse different sort of maladies stemming from the psychological, social, historical and cultural aspects by taking nine short stories into account. The title of her short story collection, *Interpreter of Maladies: Bengal, Stories of Boston and Beyond* itself, refers to her transitionality. This chapter deals with whether her fictional characters are cultural translators of their global ethnic status, and focuses on how characters from Bengal and Boston are engaged in dialogic connection in the stories revealing friendship, acculturation, alienation, and new possibilities. The cultural untranslatability which diaspora usually indicates in Lahiri's fictional characters brings out a plethora of possibilities in the myriad representations of maladies.

In **the second chapter**, I have dealt with Lahiri's *Unaccustomed Earth* which consists of eight short stories of various locations portraying the lives of first and second generation immigrants who in their respective unaccustomed earths combat to fit themselves. By bringing in psychoanalytic perspective, I have sought to demonstrate the psychological intricacies of the first generation and second generation immigrants of the stories. The chapter reveals how the diasporic characters resort to the path of 'anamnesis' in the host country and can hardly be 'amnesic' about their ancestral culture. So, the fictional characters are associated with the cross-cultural dialogues which unravel the generational gaps, in-betweenness, alienation and transitionality of her fictional characters.

In **the third chapter**, my objective is to show how cultural conflicts are evident between the first and the second generation immigrants in *The Namesake*. The chapter deals with whether the emigrants in the host country would conform to the 'forever foreigner' syndrome or would forge their entity in consonance with the ever-changing socio-politico-cultural circumstances. The cultural ambivalence, seclusion and performance of various cultural tropes such as food, and rituals bring out the heterogeneous identity of the fictional characters. Cosmopolitanism, culinary citizenship, transcendence of the cartographical epistemology and formation of the ambivalent identity like ABCD (*American born confused desi*) are the main characteristics discussed in the chapter from a critical vantage point.

In **the fourth chapter**, I have tried to exhibit how the Naxalite Movement in *The Lowland* has been used as a background to reveal the loss, gain and search for destination of her fictional characters. Mobile concurrency between the past and the present in which fictional characters are caught in has left an impact on the geopolitical contours of the host country. Such pastness appears in the novel in the ghostlike form of Udayan that traumatizes Gauri, and thus problematises her identity. It has also impacted the life of her daughter Bela and Subhas. Tension, separation, the clash between modernity and tradition, same-sex relationship are the effusion of the novel. Applying the Bakhtinian concept of Chronotope, I have attempted to forge Lahirivian chronotopes which dismantle the chronological time frame and prioritize the lived experiences of the characters. Since, the novel is an open-ended one, it indicates numerous possibilities and transitional naunces of the characters.

In **the fifth chapter**, I have attempted to track down Jhumpa Lahiri's adherence to the *Italian phase*, which refers to her shift from fiction to a non-fictional world. *In other Words* is her memoir wherein she appears as a linguistic pilgrim who is obsessed with the Italian language. She thinks herself absolutely free being immersed in the Italian language, and sometimes she is confused whether she will adhere to the Italian language or return to English. Such an ambiguity and a tension of loss and gain is anchored in her subconscious in a way that is conducive to the formation of her multiple diasporic sensibilities.

In the concluding section, Jhumpa Lahiri again attempts to emphasise the objectivity within her own self which finds resonance in her edited volume *Italian Short Stories*, "I surrendered to an inexplicable urge to distance myself, to immerse myself and to acquire a second literary formation" (IX). A few people asked her "Don't you miss English" (x). She replies "The act of translation, central to their artistic formation, was a linguistic representation of their innate hybridity" (XII). Lahiri's intention to be a cultural translator is an inherent characteristic of her own which can be traced at the beginning of her career. Hence, her present adherence to the *Italian phase* has ushered in a new journey in her life. Apropos of Lahiri's fiction and non-fiction, it is crystal clear that her take on translation is a process pertaining to the heterogeneity of diasporic subjectivity. Hence, thinking of herself as being and translating herself as an individual broaches polyphonic voices and evolves a sense from Being to Becoming. She retains her objectivity in representing her fictional characters. Her inclination to be a translator of her feelings brings out her transitionality in the true sense. Such a tendency is not only confined to her earlier essay 'Intimate Alienation', it is also evident in her recent work *Translating Myself and Others*. In her *Translating Myself and Others*, she unveils the coexistence of two separate writers within her cogito; it leads her towards self negation to come up with new creative impetus for translating and transcending any particular linguistic and cultural parameter. To Lahiri, diasporic subjectivity is a kind of journey steeped in loss, gain and destination. In fact, the spatial, cultural, and linguistic dislocation can be felt throughout her entire oeuvre: fiction and non-fiction both. This book intends to cover the translational and transnational motif of her fictional as well as non-fictional works. Geographical, cultural and social milieu vary from place to place, and Lahiri competently generates a heteroglossia of linguistic and cultural habitus which gives birth to a plurality of selves. Lahiri has rightly pinpointed how diaspora transforms its position from mobility to connectivity. She along with her fictional characters participates in such a world of connectivity; it brings out differences in the writer's approach. The continuous conflict between self and others, be it culture or language, creates ambiguity, uncertainty, transitionality, and possibility for Lahiri as well as her fictional characters.

Chapter 1:

Dialogues between multiple cultures: Reinterpreting diasporic consciousness as loss and hope in *Interpreter of Maladies: Stories of Bengal, Boston and Beyond*

Jhumpa Lahiri's *Interpreter of Maladies* (1999) literally reveals the author's bicultural entity or 'Two Lives' between which she is straddling — being a second-generation immigrant. The subtitle of the work, "Stories of Bengal, Boston and Beyond", refers to her proclivity to portray her fictional characters in the maze of cross-culturality, which surpass differences in race, age, religion, and gender. The adverb 'beyond' perceptively yields to her fictional characters an in-between space which blurs the spatio-temporal binaries. Her diasporic characters are indicating a kind of journey of deprivation, mourning for (im)possible homecomings and potential advantages for the future generation. Indeed, the nine stories in the collection transcend the stereotypical confrontation between India and the United States of America. They simply access to the path of resistance to ward themselves off the worn out tradition of Indian exoticism owing to their "not too spicy" tones (Shankar 41). Lahiri exhibits human nature in multicultural crossroads where individuals are "forced to face the great questions of change and adaptation" (Rushdie 415). Her stories capture the lives of expatriates and first-generation Americans of Indian Origin, with their alienation, sacrifices and struggles and with their desire to relate to themselves and with each other. Lahiri's stories are premised upon *ethnoscapes* of "tourists, immigrants, refugees, exiles, guest workers, and other moving groups and individuals who constitute an essential feature of the world and appear to affect the politics of (and between) nations to a hitherto unprecedented degree" (Appadurai 33). By examining the textual and structural ingredients of Lahiri's debut work, it is to be exam-

33

ined whether her characters are cultural translators of her global ethnic status, and whether the maladies they go through are diasporic metaphors, articulating the psychological, social, historical and cultural disease which are stemming from their efforts to acclimatise with their changing positions in life to find out ease by bringing in various theoretical tools. This chapter brings out multiple cross-cultural dialogues laden with loss, gain and hope which characterise diasporic individuals in the story.

In the different short-stories collected in *Interpreter of Maladies: Stories of Bengal, Boston and Beyond*, Lahiri is identifiably explicit in bringing out geopolitical, cultural and socio-political (b)order and dis(b)order through the portrayal of her fictional characters. She seeks to accentuate in "A Temporary Matter" more upon mental border between the alienated diasporic individuals Shoba and Shukumar; she does it not merely in terms of playing cultural tropes, but seeks to spot on emptiness erupting from their familial space, tending them to be morbid and alienated. They are although absorbed in tinkering the world of make-belief, but it can hardly withstand amid the blow of reality. As Skempton states:

> Alienation in Hegel is, at one stage, a manifestation of mediation, a process essential to and constitutive of human consciousness. It refers to self othering involved in self positing which is the process of differentiation that constitutes identity; if the same is the same only in so far as it is the other then the same contains the other within itself, it is itself at the same time as being other than itself. Hence, the proximity of Hegelian alienation to the notion of a fundamental difference, or difference, that underlies and undermines the full presence of identity. However, as we have seen, for Hegel, alienation and difference are characteristic as differential negativity, they are put to work in the service of the reconstitution of identity, sublated to a higher level. This higher level is a paradoxical mediated identity, an identity 'for itself', or a self conscious identity. (50)

"A Temporary Matter" is completely built upon the self-alienation from the marital entanglement between Shoba and Shukumar where reciprocity ought to be a major leitmotif. Both of them live in a tree-lined street of Boston having a profound scar in mind which seems to be emanating from the loss of their deceased offspring. They are living under the same roof, sharing meal on same table, showing affection, displaying occasional concern for each other — but to readers, it seems that they are in playacting. In fact, their family space becomes contingent where both of them are merely showing off their love and conjugal relationship which is inane at the core. Gradually they forge an invisible wall by picking themselves up from the conjugal relationship in the true sense of the term. This is somehow referring to self-amputation, which acts as a driving force between them, seems to expand the chasm of their relationship. The way Shoba "wept without sound, and whispered his name, and traced his eyebrows with a finger in the dark" (19) seems to denote the profundity of love and endearment she still perpetuates for him and the anxiety she would have to ward off before long. Individual in fact manifests a dichotomy of temporal alienation. Shoba and Shukumar is engaged with marital cord in such a way that finds its resonance in Hegelian *Unhappy consciousness*. Indeed, unhappy consciousness is opening up the path of new consciousness which can be called as the journey from consciousness to the emergence of reason. In *Sickness unto Death*, Kierkegaard examines many other senses in which an individual may fail to be reconciled to his own eternal essence, and thus enter into various states of despair. This theme of despair is resonated in the Nietzschean concept of the death of God where he did not believe in the absolute other like God. Hegel aims to reconcile with the other. Throughout self-consciousness, Hegel makes queries regarding the nature of self consciousness by the usage of the dialectic. He presents apparent contradictions, namely 'being in itself' (197) and 'being for itself' (197), and shows how said contradictions taken together consist in a higher truth, namely the 'immediate unity' or the in- and for-itself. Hegel identifies the dialectical nature of self-consciousness, focussing on the sameness and difference of self-consciousness. The term of self-consciousness, here, in Hegel's term, is 'stoicism' and 'scepticism': the unity of which is found in the 'unhappy consciousness'. He says that the stoic self-consciousness is "a being that thinks, and that... holds something to be essentially important, or true and good, in so far as it thinks it to be such" (198). The stoic self-consciousness and the sceptical self-consciousness together "maintains and creates this restless confusion" (205), recognising that it takes itself to be "wholly continent, single and separate" and, yet at the same time, universal and self-identical" (ibid. 205). Such separateness seems to be resonated in the both while the quest for self drives them to forge an individual existence; they compel themselves to be busy with any work with a view to sweeping away circumstantial sluggishness. Indeed, the ethical responsibility which is replete with love, care and affection between both, completely stands on the flimsy ground. They are absorbed in relinquishing each other by exhibiting carelessness:

> He ran his tongue over the top of his teeth; he'd forgotten to brush them that morning. It wasn't the first time. He had't left the house at all that day, or the day before. The more Shova stayed out the more she began putting an extra hours at work and taking on additional projects, the more he wanted to stay in, not even leaving to get the mail, or to buy fruit or wine at the stores by the trolley stop. (Interpreter 2)

They became "expert at avoiding each other in the three-bedroom house" (ibid. 4). Shukumar never looks forward to weekends, he is afraid that "putting on a record in his own house might be rude" (ibid. 5). "He thought of how long it had been since she looked into his eyes and smiled, or whispered his name on those rare occasions they still reached for each other's bodies before sleeping" (ibid.5). Shukumar ruminates the absence of those moments of intimacy that feature the conjugal space. Shoba chalks out a plan for the redemption of her dying self and seeks to relive in a bit different way by bringing in a game of confession; this is supposed to be the purgatory space wherein they can unlock their heart to dispense with the ongoing inertia. Invariably, maladies whatever she feels, creep into familial space through the mode of interaction. Maladies occupy a fecund ground in the gaps and apertures erupt in relationships. With the passages of time, bonding in the family space falls apart. In fact, there had been an intense bond between Shoba and Shukumar at the initial stage of their marriage while both of them had a dream of having a happy family with children. Consequently, Shoba got pregnant and was awaiting eagerly to celebrate her ensuing new born baby. A room was adorned with beautiful pictures in this connection. The arrival of the child would add bonanza to the entire family and bolster the bond a little bit more too. This is evident in Shukumar's dream of purchasing a spacious car to accommodate a bigger family:

> As the cab sped down Beacon Street, he imagined a day when he and Shoba might need to buy a station wagon of their own, to cart their children back and forth from music lessons and dentist appointments. He imagined himself gripping the wheel, as Shoba turned around to hand the children juice boxes. Once, these images of parenthood had troubled Shukumar, adding to his anxiety that he was still a student at thirty-five. But that early autumn morning the trees still heavy with bronze leaves, he welcomed the image for the first time. (3)

But the demise of the child, which becomes an *absolute other* to him, flashes upon his inward eye as a squandering effect of solitude and animates *unhappy consciousness* between the couple, resulting in the consequent self-amputation to generate individual space. Shukumar's involvement is more on his researched works than performing familial duties. He attends a seminar at Baltimore while Shoba being pregnant is fighting alone. Shukumar by severing himself from the depressing family-life is in search of something which can dismantle the existing impasse he is embroiled with. He is really conforming to the concept of "kacha Ami" ('Immature I'-a term coined by Ramakrishna) where he is propelled by his self-desire to make himself happy and also caught in the dialectics between his ethical responsibilities being a husband and his career, ultimately leading him to a disastrous synthesis. On the other hand, Shoba has a dire necessity of *the other* in the absence of her husband to stand by her during such difficult time, which propels her to call her friend Gillian for a ride to the hospital. Her mother has also come from Arizona to stay with her for two months for assisting Shoba and Shukumar especially in household works. "But you weren't even there" (9) while being uttered by Shoba's mother during the discussion over the baby's death, naturally hints at his invalid propriety of departing to Boston during the emergency period being a husband. Shukumar has unwittingly deviated from his family life being oblivious to his wife. This is indeed not a direct violence, but a sense of quiet violence emphasises 'the malady' in the family sphere.

The entire story has a sonorous movement which is found to be resonated through the exquisite interplay of light and darkness. Light is emblematic of social norms or decorum which binds people to meet the faces by wearing mask to hide one's real character and reveals it in hiding, but darkness broaches wide opportunity to express oneself more comfortable being absolutely free from the hubbub of the social code of conduct. In the dark one is absolutely alone, the effect of the presence of another self is minimised. Shoba and Shukumar think more spontaneously in the dark and confess their secret in a ritualistic way. Primarily these were about "The little ways they'd hurt or disappointed each other and themselves" (18). In the darkness they are absorbed in regenerating their affectionate bond showing gesture of affection to each other which they have forgotten for a while. However, such darkness during the power cut helps them mingle together and thereby redeem them, though ephemerally, from the onslaught of the maladies. It stands in the way of their marital progress. This has a close rapport with Jimmy and Alison's 'bear-Squirrels game' (47) in Osborne's *Look Back In Anger* (1956). Shoba's continuous persistence to carry on the game yields to her enough space for ejaculating her pent up emotions. Shukumar's turn comes to make confession, though he never longs for revealing the truth, but finally he unfurls his voice regarding his status during their upcoming offspring. He had not arrived late from Baltimore, as was believed, on the day she had delivered the stillborn baby. He had held the baby closely before they cremated him:

> Our baby was a boy," he said. "His skin was more red than brown. He had black hair on his head. He weighted almost five pounds. His fingers were curled shut, just like yours in the night. (*Interpreter* 22)

Shoba becomes restless and melancholic due to her late knowledge of Shukumar's presence at the hospital and she is completely ignorant of the fact. It is their unwillingness that generates rebuff in the proper progression of their conjugal relationships. However, the game of confession has brought them into a different plane where they discuss over the loss of their new-born baby and "wept together, for the things they now knew" (*ibid.* 22).

For the first time they have wept together because of the absent presence existence of the deceased child. In fact, the lack of their offspring helps them to be united together, which raises questions whether this is a 'temporary matter' or leading them towards final reconciliation in terms of their marital cord. In fact, the story is entirely moulded into the dialectics between light and dark, and thereby creating an intimate space, which indicates the revelation of individual conscience.

"When Mr Pirzada Came to Dine" is a story of partition which smacks of a kind of ethnic solidarity between an Indian family enrooted in American society and an Indian Immigrant namely Mr Pirzada, who arrives in America in order to pursue his Ph.D. by availing the grant provided by the Government of Pakistan. Indeed, the atmospheric tumult is looming large in India due to religio-political furore between Hindu and Muslim over the issue of yielding East Pakistan to a different entity called Bangladesh during 1971, which naturally refers to the history of partition. The entire camera angle of the story is on Mr. Pirzada and his dilapidated condition in the alien shore being a researcher and his consequent movement to and fro indicates diasporic predicament or alienation. But he has been able to get an *absolute other* in Lilia, a second-generation immigrant girl of ten years, who is narrating the entire story, and thus accentuating the plight of partition. Lilia provides Mr. Pirzada a little bit of assuage, and helps celebrate the enclave of ethnocultural solidarity by transgressing geopolitical and religious borders. Thus, she has been able to forge an umbilical cord with Mr. Pirzada. Lilia is born in Boston, a second-generation immigrant, albeit she seeks to create her individual space in the United States of America by listening to the stories of different continents in India wherein Mr Pirzada, a University professor, has a significant role to play. It not only leads them to be intimate with each other by alienating themselves from the hubbub of culture, but places their embodied existence in an imaginary world, which is nicely coloured by the shared memory of their remembered past. Lilia's family also enjoys Pirzada's association which helps ingress Indian cultural heritage into their home. Being entrenched in American culture, Lilia identifiably has an enormous interest to go beyond the geopolitical barrier. But the sudden announcement of communal carnage of 1971 provokes a divisive nationalism among the common people which consequently dismantles cultural integrity. Sarah Ahmed in her *Cultural Politics of Emotion* (2004) shows how emotion vindicates ingeniously a close rapport between body and social space and how the body has to surrender to the social taboos or prejudices. Little Lilia has to confront this trouble, but it hardly alienates herself from Pirzada (Muslim). She is devoid of socio-political turmoil of the country and intimately retains solidarity between Older Pakistan and Indian American Girl within the alien soil. Since, she is doubly alienated from her own country United States of America and also from Mr Pirzada, she consequently generates 'third space' for her.

In fact, 'third space' is "a space of radical openness, a vast territory of infinite possibilities and perils" (Soja 33). Lefebvre refers to the relation that relies between social transformation and spatial organization. Space becomes a kind of epistemological entity having a difference with cartographical or material objectivity. He believes that social space becomes an organizational tool to interfere with and determine human action. In his words,

> The fields we are concerned with are, first, the physical—nature, the cosmos; secondly, the mental, including logical and formal abstractions; and, thirdly, the social. In other words, we are concerned with logico-epistemological space, the space of social practice, the space occupied by sensory phenomena, including products of the imagination such projects and projections, symbols, and utopias. (Soja11-12)

Lahiri introduces Mr. Pirzada at the very outset of the story: "His name was Mr. Pirzada, and he came from Dacca, now the capital of Bangladesh, but then a part of Pakistan" (*Interpreter* 23). She also describes that he has, "a three-storeyed home, a lectureship in Botany at the university, a wife of twenty years, and seven daughters between ages of six and sixteen" (*ibid.* 23) in Dacca. 1971 is the age of turmoil while civil war is at work to mould East Pakistan into Bangladesh, circumstances are too sombre to be thought of where "Teachers were dragged onto streets and shot, women dragged into barracks and raped" (*ibid*. 23) by the Pakistani army.

The story is seldom a fiction, but Lahiri's personal experiences are associated with it. She utilises her childhood memories where she physically witnesses the state of mind of that Bangladeshi man who leaves her family in his native country at the time of civil war and usually loves to visit his home frequently. Even, she utters about this in her one of the interviews with Elizabeth Farnsworth as, "This story is based on a gentleman from Bangladesh who used to come to my parents' house in 1971..." and she came to know from her parents that "what his predicament was". She further explains that she "learned about his situation, which was that he was in the United States during the Pakistani civil war and his family was back in Dacca" (qtd. in Das 82). Though Mr. Pirzada has got a scholarship from the Government of Pakistan to carry on his research-work in the foreign country, but while the amount of scholarship is transmuted into dollars, it seems to be very scanty. He is not able to have a separate abode for living, stove for cooking food, television for news or entertainment and other means of amusements for sustaining his life happily in a host country. He is bound to live in a graduate dormitory. Such kind of crisis in foreign territory genuinely makes a man retrogressive and consequently returns him to his own memory related to his home culture. But his sudden familiarity with Lilia and her family provides him a space of solace. Inspite of being a Muslim, he has been able to spend time with Lilia's family by eating, and sharing his thoughts as well as nostalgic memories which are embroiled with his home culture. It is emblematic of the ethnocultural solidarity performed in the United States of America. However, his absolute alienation is to some extent redeemed with the close association of Lilia and her family. In fact, the paroxysm of mimetic violence basically stems from religious pontification between Hindu vis-à-vis Muslim debate which snatches away a lot of lives. Little Lilia can hardly understand such invisible wall which is concocted and has nothing to do with humanity; rather she appears throughout the story as the bridge maker of humanism. She unfurls,

> It made no sense to me. Mr. Pirzada and my parents spoke the same language, laughed at the same jokes, looked more or less the same. They ate pickled mangoes with their means, ate rice every night for supper with their hands. Like my parents, Mr. Pirzada took off his shoes before entering a room, chewed fennel seeds after meals as a digestive, drank no alcohol, for dessert dipped austere biscuits into successive cups of tea. (25)

While Lilia is watching television, it has been broadcasted all on a sudden,

> The united states was siding with west Pakistan, the soviet union with India and what was soon to be Bangladesh War was declared officially on 4 December, and twelve days later, the Pakistani Army, weakened by having no fight three thousand miles from their sources of supplies, surrendered in Dacca. (40)

Symbolically, during the twelve days of war Mr. Pirzada stops bringing candy, Lilia's father does not tell her to watch the news with them anymore, and even her mother refuses to serve anything more elaborate than boiled eggs with rice for dinner. Mr. Pirzada starts sleeping on their couch and they call relatives in Calcutta to learn first hand details about the situation. Actually, Mr. Pirzada now is about to return to his own country which creates a scar in his mind and Lilia, too; it denotes a symbolic partition between Lilia and him. In fact, a dialogic connection between Mr. Pirzada and Lilia has matured her up a lot. So, she cherishes her sweet memories spent with Pirzada, and his absence creates a vacuum in Lilia's mind which helps her regenerate an imaginary world. Thus, she enjoys her intimate space.

"Interpreter of Maladies" deals with the maladies, which emanate from the Indo-American couple and their Children – the Das family, who feel alienated in India as they are accustomed to American culture. However, India contains their cultural heritage too, thus resulting in a hybrid culture. In language, she follows the American tradition of spellings favouring 'color' to 'colour'. Interestingly, she utilises Indian words and phrases 'Astachala-Surya' (setting Sun), 'hanuman'(monkey), 'Nagamithunas' (act of sex), 'Villa' (place). However, Das family has a dire necessity to be healed from the socio-cultural and psychic maladies, and Mr. Kapasi, being a tour guide, takes upon him the responsibility to lead them towards the Sun Temple in Konarak, India. Lahiri defines him as a middle-aged man 'forty six years old, with a receding hair line that had gone completely silver" (*Interpreter* 45). Lahiri exquisitely delineates the dress of the family: "The family looked Indian but dressed as foreigners did, the children in stiff, brightly coloured clothing and caps with translucent visors" (*Interpreter* 44).

In fact, the discussion, which crops up from the conversation between Mrs. Das and Mr. Kapasi, revolves around her illegal offspring Bobbie, who stirs her prick of conscience, and it concomitantly, creates a chasm between her husband and her. The intimacy between Mr. Kapasi and Mrs. Das animates their loss related to their past life. In fact, Mr. Kapasi, an interpreter and meticulous observer, delves deep into the inner sanctum of Mrs. Das, and thus, he finds out the inconsistencies of her life revolving around her son Boby, who is reproduced through her extramarital affair. It reminds him of his guilt-ridden past. Mr. Kapasi becomes so intimate with her that leads him also to his memory lane fraught with the affliction of his dead son. Hence, both of their losses can be compared to a strange echo of the son in Freud's dream:

> A father had been watching day and night beside the sick bed of his child. After the child died, he retired to rest in an adjoining room, but left the door ajar so that he could look from his room into the next, where the child's body lay surrounded by tall candles. An old man, who had been installed as a watcher, sat beside the body, murmuring prayers. After sleeping for a few hours the father dreamed that the child was standing by his bed, clasping his arm and crying reproachfully: 'Father, don't you see I'm burning...Freud initially reads this dream as the wish fulfilment on the part of the father to see his child again, but then returns to the dream later in the chapter to find that it is bound up with a more profound and enigmatic wish, the desire to sleep. (qtd.in Dhingra 117-18)

Since, both of their loss helps them to be intimately alienated from this spacio-temporal barrier. In fact, as Elaine Scarry has suggested, pain destroys the world that language calls up, and Lahiri implies that the task of interpreting this pain falls on the individual who lives as one removed from the trauma. As Scarry notices in *The Body in Pain* "because the person in pain is so ordinarily bereft of the resources of speech, it is not surprising that the language of pain should sometimes be brought into being by those who are not themselves in pain but who can speak on behalf of those who are" (6). Mr. Kapasi who has been deployed by Lahiri, has a very ingenious purpose to analyse or interpret the manifold losses. It has been manifested through many texts. The role of Mr. Kapasi is very significant as he must narrate the bodily symptoms of the patients belonging to multilingual cultures to the doctor, who is referring to his ethical responsibility towards the patients. In a conversation with Mrs. Das, she says

> These patients are totally dependent on you...in a way more dependent on you than the doctor...for example, you could tell the doctor that the pain felt like a burning, not straw. The patient would never know what you had told the doctor, and the doctor wouldn't know that you had told the wrong thing. It's a big responsibility. (*Interpreter* 51)

In fact, Mr. Kapasi seems to act not only as an interpreter of physical pain but psychic pain, too. His role as an interpreter of maladies cannot specify his territory, but compels him to ingress into the inner sanctum of human minds, too, which has been reflected during the conversation between him and Mrs. Das. Such role of Mr. Kapasi can be compared to Claude Levi-Strauss's delineation of 'shaman' which he relates to the analyst:

> The shaman provides the sick woman with a language by means which unexpressed, and otherwise inexpressible, psychic states can immediately be expressed. And it is the transition to this verbal stage...which induces the release of the physiological process, that is, the reorganization in a favourable direction...In this respect, the shamanistic cure lies on the borderline between our contemporary physical medicine...and such psychological therapies as psychoanalysis. (198)

Levi-Strauss's narration of the work of the shamanistic analyst is akin to Freud's delineation of the work of mourning, Caruth's theory of trauma, and in Lahiri's collection, the work of the author. The Shaman, according to Levi-Strauss, yields to the woman the linguistic ability to express the otherwise inexpressible. The deliberation of their language leads them towards the process of 'favourable direction'. In fact, this is a process which has a consonance with Freud's idea of mourning. Freud's concept of mourning is deriving from the loss of the object which needs to be concretised through language to provide loss a salubrious identity and thus loss is reorganised and given a subjectivity. Whenever, such process is fulfilled the "ego becomes free and uninhabited again" (166) resonating Levi-Strauss's theory of the "release of the physiological process, that is, the reorganization in a favourable direction". The interaction between Mrs. Das and Mr. Kapasi refers to the intersection between literature and psychoanalysis. As Lacan suggests, "the passing of psychoanalytic theory is an imperative that turns between traumatic repetition and the ethical burden of survival" (*Unclaimed Experience* 107-108). Mrs. Das unlocks her secret of infidelity to Mr. Kapasi in a confession:

> We married when we were still in college. We were in high school when he proposed. We went to the same college, of course. Back then we couldn't stand the thought of being separated. Not for a day...As a result of spending all her time with [him], she continued, [I] did not make many close friends. There was no one [to] confide in about him at the end of a difficult day. (*Interpreter* 63)

Such lamentation is denoting her sole malady which is mitigated by dint of Mr. Kapasi. In fact, Bobbie, who is the illegitimate son of Mrs Das is in danger and is attacked by the monkeys as she did not share her puffed rice to anyone:

> Surrounded by a group of monkeys, over a dozen of them, pulling at his T-shirt with their long black fingers. The puffed rice Mrs. Das had spilled was scattered at his feet, raked over by the monkeys' hands. The boy was silent, his body frozen, swift tears running down his startled face. (*ibid.* 67-68)

Mrs. Das then pleads help to rescue her son from Mr Kapasi by proclaiming "Do something, for God's sake, do something!" (*ibid.*68). Mrs. Das's desire to help her child somehow leads her to be engaged in performing her motherly affection and awakens her ever-dwindling motherly feelings in a new way. Mr. Kapasi and Mrs. Das generate their own world of memory teemed with a loss, which helps them to be intimately alienated from the onslaught of time and space. The Interpreter always assumes an in-betweenness or *untranslatability* to express the multilingual feelings of different people, which accentuates his queerness too, but both Mr Kapasi and Mrs Das have been suffering from a queerness of the same kind which reinforces their intimacy and friendship.

In "A Real Durwan", Bori Maa feels afoul of the Government rule enacted during 1971 which bears with the divide and rule policy and consequently, she becomes the victim of the circumstances. She has come across forced migration and lost her wealth, status what she belonged to earlier, now she is in a peripheral position, and thereby articulating her otherness. She being the real Durwan, gives her full effort for retaining her minimum existence in the society. She looks after the home at her best, but sudden theft of the bucket conduces furore against her because she is thought to be the main culprit of it. It really mortifies her and pushes her to move to her past life which is replete with wealth, money what she used to possess. Now she is really alienated from the society and anticipates her alienation with the stigma which widens her ambit to live her own world intimately via memory and present stark reality of the society.

Everything happens in this material life in accordance with the disciplinary process, which is usually manipulated by the state power: it makes man a living being into its own specific object which has a close rapport with the Aristotelian notion that 'man is by nature a political animal' (Aristotle 28-29), it invariably segregates the private or domestic life and the political life. In fact, what Foucauldian modern democracy denotes is nothing but the absorption of the living being into a subject of the political power. It actually connotes the difference between classical democracy and modern democracy. Modern democracy begins with the liberation of 'Zoe' and it is constantly trying to transform its own bare life into a way of life, and to find, so to speak, the bios of 'Zoe'. It actually wants to put the freedom and happiness of men into play in the very place — 'bare life' that marked their subjection. This is in fact a never-ending fissure between domestic life and political life like the body is experiencing mind and the mind is experiencing body in Agambenian sensibility. Both the domestic and political life is adjoined together and one's own private sphere is under the surveillance of the State power/state of exception. Bori Maa seems to refer to such context where being refugee she is always under the surveillance of State power, and thus, she represents the 'bare life'.

Thomas Hobbes and John Locke's concept of the state as a body-politic in which the bodies of the citizenry combine into undivided body of the sovereign, with whom they form a single unity or will. And security which the nation or state provides is nothing but a kind of political technology that tantalizes two linked techniques of social production and regulation: totalizing power, of the kind put to use by states over vast areas, economics and populations; and individualizing power, which works at the level of individuals and souls, on their bodies and minds. The protection is less a desired end of politics that drums up horror and pleasures, coercion and desire in equal measures, through a linked system of language, force, administration and freedom. Security is both a mode of administrative and governmental action-bureaucratic, ideological, military and economic and a system of 'truth' that move people's hearts, forging their identities, feelings and hopes. Security is an ideal state promise of perfect state safety and smoothness, providing military force and so on, but that security which emanates from the state, explores the exploitation in terms of the economy and sexuality, too. The State has always a kind of Panopticon gaze at people, who are under their umbrella. Boori Maa has an ethical responsibility to perform her duties to the apartment as a durwan and ensure the security. Boori Maa is socially insecure or ostracised as the theft of the bucket that leads her to the position of marginality: "Boori Ma's mouth is full of ashes. But that is nothing new. What is new is the face of this building. What a building like this needs is a real durwan" (*Interpreter* 82). In fact, the societal stratification, which is emanating from caste and class, seems to rob of her voices and turns her into an insignificant cog, who is always uttering "believe me or don't believe me" (83). She refers to her border anxiety: "anxiety and fear create the effects of borders, and the effect of that which we are not. The transgression of the border is required in order for it to be secured as a border in the first place. As such security involves the securing of 'the not', which paradoxically requires the insecurity of "the not" (Ahmed 76). The borders of the collective causing continuous threat to her psyche which turns her into a *docile body*.

> By conceptualizing the interlocking of bodies and discursive regimes, Foucault enables us to understand the process of subject constitution in modern society. As a body subject tó modern, colonial technology of power-knowledge, the colonized should be produced as a new body and mind with certain skills, characteristics, and form; she/he needs to be remade. But to understand this remapping and re-territorialization, we need to position the body of the other within a frame which can account for it as a historical and cultural effect of power. The other's particular mode of corporeality is an important site for colonial inscriptions of power. (Yegenoglu 117)

Hence, Boori Maa's *lived body* creates her existence on her own and her unfulfilled desire is nicely meted out through her stories tinged with her past memories: "So she garbled facts. She contradicted herself. She embellished almost everything. But her rants were so persuasive, her feting so vivid, that it was not so easy to dismiss her" (72). Indeed, Boori Ma, who connotes the concept of the Bengali word *chinnamul* (literally 'torn-rooted') in the context of diaspora or partition, celebrates her alienation in this way: "Bechareh, She probably constructs tales as a way of mourning the loss of her family, was the collective surmise of most of the wives" (*Interpreter* 72).

"Sexy" explores the immigrant experience in the U.S.A. which is tinged with corporeal mechanism, and it devours South Asian immigrants' entity. Dev, a Bengali immigrant, in the story, becomes the victim of epicurean aspect of life, which stems from America in the guise of Miranda, the representative of gross materiality in the story. He gets sucked into her in spite of being married which is attuned to Fanon's notion "By loving me she proves that I am worthy of white love. I am loved like a white man. I am a white man" (Fanon63). Dev being an Indian migrant has been able to attract the attention of an American lady Miranda, who tends to generate the ground of extramarital affair and seems to reincarnate neo-orientalism in this connection. The question of morality and immorality stands on the vague ground. In fact, "longing for the pleasure that has led the white west to sustain a romantic fantasy of the "primitive" and the concrete search for a real primitive paradise, whether that location be a country or a body, a dark continent or dark flesh, perceived as the perfect embodiment of that impossibility" (Hooks 370). This is nicely deciphered while Miranda being swayed away by the Indian culture repeatedly tries to mend her accent of 'Indianness':

> What causes Miranda to feel 'numb' rather than 'hot'-is her realization that despite her best efforts to try on the accents of 'Indianness'-to Indianize her name, to learn the Bengali alphabet, etc.— she cannot approximate the gendered and racialized logics of Madhuri Dixit's body. (101)

Dixit's sexy body becomes a global brand of South Asian public culture which relegates occidental beauty of Miranda; it subverts the representation of the 'orient' by the White western culture by providing a little bit of privilege to the orient beauty in the story. Dev's description of her wife resonates the resemblance of her wife with the Indian film actress Madhuri Dixit, and the unseen beauty of Dev's wife augments sexual jealousy of Miranda towards his wife. Bell Hooks proclaims in his *Eating The Other*

> The desire to make contact with those bodies deemed Other, with no apparent will to dominate, assuages the guilt of the past, even takes the form of a defiant gesture where one denies accountability and historical connection. Most importantly, it establishes a contemporary narrative where the suffering imposed by structures of domination on those designated Other is deflected by an emphasis on seduction and longing where the desire is not to make the Other over in one's image but to become the Other. (369)

However, Dev's wife feels intimacy towards her home, so she goes there and it really gives Dev enough scope to be interpellated into American corporeal subject. His wife enjoys his intimacy from her home and maintains relationship with her husband through the phone calls. His too much association and intimacy with the host culture dissociates him from his own culture or root. On the other hand, Laxmi's cousin's husband is also engaged in another western woman. Such scenario extrapolates Indian males and their absorption into the host culture completely; it rescinds their moral baggage tethered to Indian culture. Although, east and west initially tries to engage themselves intimately across the continents, it leads to cultural alienation. This very story sharply states that sex or biological determinism cannot be the ultimate trope for establishing a conjugal relationship, rather mind matters, which is completely embedded in East / West dialectic represented by the female and male characters, respectively. Rohin, the small boy, after observing Miranda proclaims, "You are sexy" (*Interpreter* 107); it represents a close rapport with Dev's words, she answers in return "It means loving someone you don't know" (107). Rohin asks his mother whether the other women are sexy, and it, consequently, generates the question of propriety in her mind, "How could you love as woman you don't even know?" (*ibid.* 108). Being immensely mortified for what she has done, she is "gazing at its giant pillars and its massive dome, and at the clear-blue sky spread over the city" (*ibid.*110). However, to be mournful is nothing but tends Miranda to nourish "imperialist nostalgia" (defined by Renato Rosaldo in *Culture and Truth* as "nostalgia, often found under imperialism, where people mourn the passing of what they themselves have transformed" or as "a process of yearning for what one has destroyed that is a form of mystification") often obscures contemporary cultural strategies deployed not to mourn but to celebrate the sense of a continuum of *Primitivism*" (Hooks 369). Such dichotomous or oppositional intimacy in terms of culture broaches intricacies and ultimate alienation, too.

"Mrs Sen" is another short story of Lahiri which is adroitly juxtaposing polyphonic voices of Mrs. Sen, an immigrant spouse of a Professor on the alien shore like the U.S.A., and Eliot, an eleven-year-old-boy of the U.S.A. Mrs. Sen is a stranger to Eliot, and Eliot is also a stranger to Mrs. Sen in terms of culture and habits. But their strangeness has added beauty to the story as well. It appears that their souls have evaporated from this cartographical epistemology to make themselves realise about their individual cultures. Both of them, with all their cultural varieties, ask for an affectionate bond. But this bond falls apart due to their rigorous cultural binary which is embedded in their subconscious mind. However, Mrs Sen always seeks to materialise the absence of Indigenous culture and it acts upon her as an 'aura'; it gets reflected through her inclination to fish, Indian classical music, crowd and above all her inadvertent car driving as well. While she asks Eliot: "Eliot, If I began to scream right now at the top of my lungs, would someone else come?" (*Interpreter* 116). She compares the isolation in America, which helps her return to her home in India where one would have to "just raise your voice a bit, or express grief or joy of any kind, and one whole neighbourhood and half of another has come to share the news, to help with arrangements" (*ibid.* 116). Eliot also gets the opportunity to know the Indian culture by interacting with her, but he possesses a very low opinion regarding Indian Culture, too. It simply articulates how association leads to dissociation and also refers to the concept of 'Sudesibad' or 'neo nativism' as proposed by G.N. Devy. In fact, the dialectic between marga (mainstream) and desi (local/regional) is conducive to the formation of 'Sudesibad' or 'neo nativism'. In fact, food becomes a very vital ploy through which she can only retain her subjectivity as the practitioner of neo-nativism:

> She took whole vegetables between her hands and hacked them apart: Cauliflower cabbage, butternut squash. She splits things in half, then quarters, speedily producing florets, cubes, slices, and shreds. She could peel a potato in seconds. At times she sat cross-legged, at times with legs splayed, surrounded by an array of colanders and shallow bowls of water in which she immersed her chopped ingredients. (*ibid.* 114)

Her proper caring of Eliot and chopping vegetables, craving for fresh fish and blade denote Cultural amnesia, which result in celebration of ethnic consciousness while she feels unaccustomed to the host culture: "She had brought the blade from India, where apparently there was at least one in every household. Whenever there is a wedding in the family", she told Eliot one day, "or a large celebration of any kind, my mother sends out word in the evening for all the neighbourhood women to bring blades just like this one, and then they sit in an enormous circle on the roof of our building, laughing and gossiping and slicing fifty kilos of vegetables through the night. Her profile hovered protectively over her work, a confetto of cucumber, eggplant and onion skins heaped around her" (*ibid.* 115). A strong sense of ethnic solidarity is hinted at here, which invariably leads her to say "Everything is there" [in India] (*ibid.* 113). G.N Devy believes if cultural amnesia dismantles the immediate past, it helps as a strategy to preserve the self-respect of the dominated culture as well as to gain approval from the dominating culture. Devy refers to the Freudian concept:

> The colonizing force is seen in the role of a present hated and feared and imitated by the colonized culture, which starts perceiving itself as a child who fears its own impotency and fantasizes about the productive power of the parent. Then, the intimidated child engages itself in acts to win the approval of the parent to enable itself to define its own new identity. (qtd.in Devy 125)

At the time of cross-cultural encounter between Mrs. Sen and the host culture, she feels queer and seeks to relive her primordial consciousness associated with her home-culture by performing her food habits, which gradually creep into her lived body. Ahmed writes in her chapter "Queer Feelings", "To preserve an attachment is...to keep one's impressions alive, as aspects of one's self that are both oneself and more than oneself, as a sign of one's debt to others" (160). Keeping impressions alive means maintaining one's own history, and in Mrs Sen's case, her difference in the American context; the 'debt to other' refers not only to the Indian community of the past, which forged her identity, but ,perhaps, to Eliot, too. The story finishes with the disintegration of the relationship between Mrs. Sen and the young boy that fossilises the isolation each feels, but the car accident by Mrs. Sen indicates possible danger for Eliot which is why Eliot is put aside by her mother from the clutches of Mrs Sen. Hence, this is a dialogic relationship between them, which conveys a mark of divisions so far as history is concerned. Mrs. Sen's intimacy with her own culture and sharing it on the different plane with foreign person, Eliot, evokes her intimate alienation not only through culture but psychology as well.

"The Blessed House" comprises of Sanjeev and Twinkle, newly married couple who are so distanced from their life, they are not willingly married to each other, and the two souls are united together by the direction of their parents on the Indian cultural parlance. But after their marriage, as they become intimate more and more with each other, they are separated from each other too, having a close acquaintance with Vijay Mishra's words "All diasporas are unhappy, but every diaspora is unhappy in its own way" (Mishra 3). Both Sanjeev and Twinkle have brought unhappiness with tiny matters which generates a complete discord in their relationship. Twinkle is tantamount to light and she adores Christ's figure which bears a cultural shock to Sanjeev. Sanjeev seems to be interpellated into the subject of the Indian cultural heritage. Twinkle being a second-generation immigrant intimates to her own world and Sanjeev being a first-generation immigrant himself alienates from her probably out of his inferior complexity. In fact, Twinkle is quite handy in coping with the both cultures which is yielding to her a hybrid identity. This house moving allegorically can be interpreted as a movement in the United States of America. These two characters are standing on complete antipodes. Twinkle's parents have long lived in California and so, she is an American of Indian origin. It displays actually the disconnection between the first and second generation immigrants in the United States. Being unable to adhere to such socio-cultural construction, he debilitates his spirit consequently. He himself alienates and becomes intimate with his own world as if he is "precariously lodged within an episteme of real or imagined displacement, self-imposed sense of exile" (Mishra 3).

In "The Treatment of Bibi Halder", Bibi Halder's life becomes groggy due to the misogynistic nature of society which is deemed as 'sado-rituals' (coined by Mary Daly); it invariably leads to the attrition of women folk. Social taboos emanating from the patrimony appear with their moral baggage to swallow the voices of an individual lady. This prejudiced society appears with much more severity to encroach upon one's private life and Bibi Halder is no exception: that lady is found pregnant, having no husband. As a matter of fact, the prejudiced society thinks her to be a burden, who should be married off at any cost to legitimise her position in the society, lest she can be treated as an omen or evil to the society.

Mary Daly begins her discussion of the sado-ritual by discussing the so-called importance of ritual, in general, to all of our lives. The myths of the masters, those myths upon which our society is built, are perpetuated through rituals. The continuous repetition of the myth functions to provide common experiences that will help tie the members to one another and to all those members of the group who came before...the mythic Truth of the patriarchal society in which we all live: men are superior, and women are inferior. Daly uses the pre-patriarchal and patriarchal myths to demonstrate how the myth is designed to model social expectation and attitude, and it is repeated in order to affirm the desired social expectation and attitude; thus, those who act in accordance with the myth are rewarded, and those who defy the myth are punished. (Hogland and Frye 136-37)

Bibi Halder seems to epitomise such miserable position. Initially, Bibi Halder, who is depicted as a subaltern character in the Indian ritualistic society, finds herself alienated after the demise of her father. So, she seeks to get married to somebody and it seems to be the only antidote for her. She appears as an outcast in the family and society. She is supposed to be the reason of illness for Mrs Halder's baby. Bibi Halder's condition reminds us of witch-burning society of Europe during the sixteenth and seventeenth century as mentioned by Mary Dally. In the Indian context we can have ample references to it. But she imbibes within herself Nietzschean affirmation or 'will to power' by uprooting herself from the societal space and plunges into her own world in which she leads her life with her baby, independently. To be intimate towards her own life, she pays a deaf ear to the androcentric society and this is nothing but her odyssey from 'Dionysian' to 'Apollonian' world. Thus, she anticipates her alienation which provides her courage to move on against the onslaughts of time.

"The Third and Final Continent" is invariably hinting at a buffer zone where the first- and second-generation immigrants are caught in cross cultural encounter, resulting in transgression which has nothing to do with the geopolitical and special determinisms. After the enactment of Immigration and Naturalization act in 1965, lots of people go to American, the Nation of nations, for finding them established and educated like that of the unnamed narrator in the story who proclaims:

I lived in London, in Finsbury Park, in a house occupied entirely by penni-
less Bengali bachelors like myself, at least a dozen and sometimes more, all
struggling to educate and establish ourselves abroad. (172)

He has been able to garner a full time job in a library at the M.I.T.
The unnamed narrator can also relish the taste of his own home
culture in Massachusetts while he says: "We lived three or four to
a room, shared a single icy toilet, and took turns cooking pots of
egg curry, which we ate with our hands on a table covered with
newspapers" (*Interpreter* 173). This has a strong reference to the
formation of desi culture or Bengali ethnic culture within the host
culture: a kind of solidarity being forged amidst the emigrants
who are considered as 'model minority' in the foreign territory.
The ethnic solidarity has been accentuated in the story in such a
way that seems to find out their ease in spite of being a foreigner
in America in terms of their culture and habits. However, the unnamed narrator in order to fulfil her marital purpose, goes to Kolkata for performing her marital rituals. Such docile housewife
Mala is shown to be identifiably Indian Bengali in her behaviour
and etiquette. She "could cook, knit, embroider, sketch land-
scapes, and recite poems by Tagore" (*ibid.* 181). Having had emi-
grated to the U.S.A, she understandably feels alienated until becoming acclimatised with the foreign culture. Mala's outlook and
identity is problematical, especially when she feels that she is as-
similating herself well into the American culture, she comes to be
praised by the westerner, Mrs. Croft, who praises her dresses and
manners, proclaiming her to be 'a perfect lady' (*ibid.* 195), even as
Helen Craft, the American daughter, wears a short dress. Mrs.
Craft's idea of getting a Westerner 'arrested' for wearing 'mini-
skirts' is, in fact, Lahiri's eulogy of Bengali socio-cultural ethos.
Mrs. Croft's insistence on Covered dress code connotes her Victo-
rian conservatism and this is to some extent related to Indigenous
culture as well. Lahiri's portrayal of Mrs Craft reinforces Bengali
ethnic culture a bit, which seems to triumph over American culture.

In fact, Lahiri's choice to conclude the story is quite strategic
while she depicts the struggle to accommodate and survive across

Asia, Europe and finally North America. The narrator retains a balance with his own life through his role of fatherhood and thus being physically and emotionally more mature man. He further admits that by means of visiting their birthplace, now and then both he and his wife are "American citizens now" (*Interpreter* 197). But when he and Mala will be dead, uncertainties would be cropping up from his "alone and unprotected son" (*ibid.* 197). This has a close consonance with Clifford's notion,

> this constitutive suffering coexists with the skills of survival: strength in adaptive distinction, discrepant cosmopolitanism and stubborn visions of renewal. Diaspora consciousness lives loss and hope as a defining tension. (312)

In fact, "The Third and Final Continent" ends with a positive connotation — it celebrates the success of the ethics of a 'model minority' of South Asian mobs as emphasised by Lahiri. However, their journey from *Roots to Routes* is not an easy one, rather surrounded, by their past memories resulting in forging a semi Bengali home culture within the host culture. The story is completely based on the spatio-temporal dislocation: a matter of transgression among a woman born in 1863 and a boy growing up on the cusp of the third millennium. Thus, alienation, pain, struggling and uncertainty about the impending future are knotted ingeniously.

In "The Third and Final Continent", the narrator has a propensity to be intimate with his own culture — that is, the Indian Culture by practicing ethno-cultural habits like eating egg-curry and walking barefoot in the house and similarly maintains modernity, too, by giving his wife's direction to follow the modern dress code abandoning 'sari': "And too turns cooking pots of egg curry, which we ate with our hands on a table covered with newspapers" (*Interpreter* 650). "There is no need to cover your head, 'I said'. I don't mind. It does not matter here" (*ibid,* 650). In fact, the narrator cuts himself out from any specific location and culture and thus being intimate in his own world. He thus really assumes an in-between space and the title of "The Third and Final Continent" itself justifies such multiple locations.

Indeed, Jhumpa Lahiri competently delineates various types of maladies of her fictional characters who are caught in dialectic and differences and thereby providing transnational nuances to her characters. The theme of alienation, multiple locations, cultural clashes, quest for individual self are prominent in the nine short stories exhibiting the basic characteristics of the diaspora. Cultural cross-pollination identifies her proclivity to dismantle the narrow nationalism and reveals her 'beyondness' in these short stories as well.

Chapter 2:

Locational antipathy: A transnational mash up of emotion and culture in *Unaccustomed Earth*

Indian immigrants in the United States of America always occupy a distinct position with their specific purpose of attaining their material needs. And the United States of America stands stiff with a stature like a nation of nations who exhibits its hospitality, if not unconditional, and puts diasporic first- and second-generation immigrants into a sheer conflict in terms of emotion, culture and location in general and Jhumpa Lahiri in particular. In fact, the enactment of *The Immigration and National Act* of 1965 and *The Hart Celler Act* of 1965, which debunk racial and national barriers in the United States of America, open up immense possibilities for people to arrive in the United States of America and arise with their American dreams. However, the transplanted identity which Lahiri seeks to unravel by referring to Hawthorne's "The Custom House" at the very beginning of *Unaccustomed Earth* identifies her locational antipathy and nonconformity to her ancestral culture too:

> Human nature will not flourish, any more than a potato, if it be planted and replanted, for too long a series of generations, in the same worn-out soil. My children have had other birthplaces, and so far as their fortunes may be within my control, shall strike roots into unaccustomed earth. (Hawthorne 11)

Lahiri's introduction to Hawthorne in this connection is not only meant to reconcile with Hawthorne entirely, but to dissent with his notion of the complete dominance of parents over their children. She believes that the children who are born and brought up in the United States of America, are usually caught up in cultural crossroads and seem to be more accustomed to their birth place and cultural habits than performing their ancestral culture practised by their parents or first-generation immigrants. It seems to be attuned to Roland Barthes's "The Death of the Author" which refers to the repudiation of the authorial hegemony upon his or her works. He compares the author and his creation with father and son relationship where he seeks to jeopardise father's dominance over the child by rendering freedom to the child. Lahiri, in her second short-story-collection *Unaccustomed Earth*, explicates such freedom of the children of the second-generation immigrants who are yet to be regulated by their ancestral culture to which their parents belong and also denotes the transnational mash up of emotion, culture and human nature resulting in a prolonged sense of loss and alienation. In fact, *Unaccustomed Earth* (2008) consists of eight short stories of various locations depicting the lives of first- and second-generation immigrants who in their respective unaccustomed earths combat to fit themselves.

In the first short-story of the collection — "Unaccustomed Earth" — Ruma being a second-generation-immigrant is afraid of her father's encroachment upon her private sphere where she is lingering for adhering to the American culture more than her ancestral culture as replicated by her father's abrupt arrival. In fact, she is frantically trying to disown herself from the memories of her mother and motherland which seems to generate an existential threat for her in American culture. In 'Hell-Heaven', the second story in this collection, Lahiri hints at a sense of loneliness and alienation which Pranab Chakroborty, a graduate student at M.I.T. in Cambridge (Massachusetts), is embroiled with on account of his homesickness. "Once in a Lifetime", the first story in the second section of the book, focuses on the growing intimacy of two families entrenched in their shared cultures and similar experience of fitting into a cultural mould. Hence, all the eight short stories in this collection are smacking of spatial and cultural transplantation which is conducive to the formation of identity crisis, spatial tension and alienation.

Lahiri's "Unaccustomed Earth" represents a pastiche of memories where space and place coalesces and sometimes overlaps, generating a tension in the mind of Ruma, the second-generation-immigrant, who has adored her kitchen with maternal care and memories and feels unwilling to share her private space with her father. Lahiri's story deals with different aspects of diasporic spatial politics, playing vital roles in identity building. Ruma is a second-generation-immigrant whose identity is really under threat while her father is about to reach her place. Her memories are associated with her mother and motherland. And they meet face to face to have provided her new identity in Seattle. Indeed, "Unaccustomed Earth" is about the dislocation and relocation of the diasporic individuals, resulting in spatial overlapping which Ruma faces and moves from one spatial matrix to another. Ruma is the cameo of thousands of Bengali women who is busy to focus on her continuous adherence to the foreign land where she has to migrate, cope with the unaccustomed world and dream of forging home in that new place. So, Ruma's predicament knows no bound:

> Where is home? On the one hand, 'home' is a mythic place of desire in the diasporic imagination. In this sense it is a place of no return, even if it is possible to visit the geographical territory that is seen as the place of 'origin'. On the other hand, home is also the lived experience of a locality. Its sounds and smells, its heat and dust, balmy summer evenings, or the excitement of the first snowfall, shivering winter evenings, sombre grey skies in the middle of the day...all this, as mediated by the historically specific everyday of social relations. (Brah 188-89)

In Lahiri's story, home does not only refer to Ruma's migration experiences, but also many other things. Ruma's father has retired from a pharmaceutical company, and after his retirement, he has set out for different places all over the world. He has consciously chosen to get himself aloof from his country. He sends Ruma postcards very often: "The postcards showed the facades of churches, stone fountains, crowded piazzas, terracotta rooftops mellowed by the late afternoon sun" (*Unaccustomed* 3). Lahiri very ingeniously has deployed the mechanism of postcards here which are quite instrumental in cropping up the secret of Ruma's father's nascent romance with Mrs. Bagchi. In fact, postcards sent by her father from various countries become the container of different spatial locations which seem to collide with Ruma's challenge to constitute her nest in Seattle. The variety of postcards from multi-

ple countries sent by her father certainly explicates his proneness
to retain a distance from his country out of his emotional engagement with the place where his wife dies. He badly wants to be a
stranger in this connection to get rid of her wife's place and memories. The dreary postcards never connote the virtual existence of
her father: "But there was never a sense of her father's presence in
those places" (ibid. 4). However, postcards are the only means of
correspondence: "The postcards were the first pieces of mail Ruma had received from her father. In her thirty-eight years he'd
never had any reason to write to her" (ibid. 4). On the other hand,
the postcards bearing the imprints of her father's arrival seem to
be threatening to her as she is profoundly absorbed in building up
her new identity by immuring herself within the four walls in her
new home.

Ruma plans to quit her job after the birth of her first child
Akash to submit herself to the will of her family life. Lahiri here
seems to suggest an inclination of the diasporic individuals who
are often trying to forget their nation and home in order to create
their new identity in a new soil, abandoning the anxiety of influence of their motherland. As Alison Blunt says,

> Unlike the sites and landscapes of memory that are located and refigured
> in the past and present, the spaces of home invoked by nostalgia remain
> more elusive and distant. (Blunt 14)

Ruma's crave for having acquired alternative identity in a foreign
territory going beyond the memories of her motherland is a direct
challenge to the conventional notion of regenerating the concept
of imaginary homeland and also to exonerate herself from ghettoization. This is why she feels awkward for her father's impending
arrival at her place: "Ruma feared that her father would become a
responsibility, an added demand, continuously present in a way
she was no longer used to"(Unaccustomed 7).In fact, the way she
has shown her dedication and patience amidst the hospitality and
hostility in a new soil to constitute her private space, seems to be
on the verge of extinction: "It would mean an end to the family
she'd created on her own: herself and Adam and Akash, and the
second child that would come in January, conceived just before

the move" (*ibid.*7). In fact, such anxiety of Ruma metaphorically can be termed as castration anxiety which seems to destroy the homing desire to which diasporic people usually belong. The loss of home is usually embedded in the unconscious mind of diasporic people which helps them long for returning to their home by means of their imaginative fiat and it consequently appears to be deterrent to the formulation of their lived space performing alien culture in alien country. In fact, cultural shock, threat of nostalgia and homing desire are tending them to abjure their new identity in a foreign place. Diasporic people always strive for having solidarity in terms of culture and language in order to essentialise their ethnic enclave and thus being able to realise their cultural and spatial alienation in new location. But Ruma continuously seeks to avert such ethnic solidarity which is very much looming large in her mind through her mother figure but the abrupt appearance of her father seems to feel her castrated; general propensity of a diasporic individual is to go for oedipal romance with his or her home which is replaced by Ruma's oedipal tryst with host country here. So while her father sends her message of his arrival in her place, she feels uneasy to accept it. Her father is the metonymic figure representing ancestral cultural baggage—the site of her lived past memories which invariably ingress in her present and threaten her severely:

> The sight of her father's rental car, a compact maroon sedan, upset her, freshly confirming the fact that she lived on a separate coast thousands of miles from where she grew up, a place where her parents knew no one, where neither of her parents, until today, had set foot. The connections her family had formed to America, her parents' circle of Bengali friends in Pennsylvania and New Jersey, her father's company, the schools Ruma and Romi had gone through, did not exist here. (*ibid.* 11)

Ruma desperately tries to settle her existence in the alien shore, but still feels alienated as she is always propelled by her mother and trying to emulate the paths of her mother at the time of her recreating home within the foreign territory exactly like that of a person belonging to the foreign culture. Ruma used to say "her mother, trained all her life to serve her husband first, would never consider such a thing." (*ibid.*16). She also seeks to prove herself to be successful in furnishing her home in the alien culture in front of her father as her mother usually did, but the subtle difference is that both are belonging to a different world:

> It was a room Ruma was most proud of, with its soapstone counters and cherry cupboards. Showing it off her father, she felt self conscious of her successful life with Adam, and at the same time she felt a quiet slap of rejection, gathering, from his continuous silence, that none of it impressed him. (*ibid.* 16)

Both Ruma and her father belong to two inimical worlds, while Ruma is too much concerned with her family or private space, but her father is having a zeal to roam various countries after the demise of his wife:

> He had never visited the Pacific Northwest, never appreciated the staggering breadth of his adopted land. He had flown across America only once before, the time his wife booked tickets to Calcutta on Royal Thai Airlines, via Los Angeles, rather than travelling east as they normally did. (*ibid.* 8)

In this story Ruma's dead mother has a very vital role to play who acts as an absent presence existence. The very beginning line of the story testifies to it brilliantly:

> After her mother's death, Ruma's father retired from the pharmaceutical company where he had worked for many decades and began travelling in Europe, a continent he'd never seen. (*ibid.*1)

In fact, the demise of her mother may signify the disappearance of her homing desire. Mother and motherland somehow becomes synonymous with Ruma's imagination, where the absent-presence entity of her mother strengthens her movement enough:

> There were times Ruma felt closer to her mother in death than she had in life, an intimacy born simply of thinking of her so often, of missing her. But she knew that this was an illusion, a mirage, and that the distance between them was now infinite, unyielding. (*ibid.*27)

Ruma feels many a time a deep-seated attachment with her mother and it becomes quite acute while her mother expires. She always at the back of her mind tries to make herself like that of her mother. Ruma, as Lahiri writes,

... tried to think of her parents' house transformed this way. She imagined
a wall in the dining room broken down, imagined speaking to her mother
on the telephone, her mother complaining as the workmen hammered and
drilled. (ibid.46)

The death of her mother exorcises Ruma tremendously which gets
its resonance through her resemblance with her deceased mother:
"I am working, Baba. Soon I'll be taking care of two children, just
like Ma did" (ibid. 46). Ruma's father is also surprised with the
appearance of her daughter sounding as if her wife:

Something about his daughter's appearance had changed; she now resem-
bled his wife so strongly that he could not bear to look at her directly. The
first glimpse of her earlier, standing on the lawn with Akash, had nearly
taken his breath away. Her face was now, as his wife's had been, and the
hair was beginning to turn grey at her temples in the same way, twisted
with an elastic band into a loose knot. (ibid.27)

In fact, the second generation immigrant Akash who is very much
akin to foreign culture, can hardly call up her grandmother: "I
don't remember Dida...I don't remember it, She died" (ibid.23). On
the contrary, Ruma is out and out mortified by the absence of her
mother and her father's secret romance with Mrs. Bagchi which
seem to be accentuated a lot by the presence of her father at her
home, igniting her to be intimate with her past.

"Hell-Heaven" is a second story of this collection exhibiting
how the Bengali immigrants are alienated from themselves in
spite of having cultural semblances, the generational gap between
the first- and second-generation-immigrants and the continuous
negotiation and renegotiation between eastern and western cultural milieu, attributing cultural divergences to the story. However, two Bengali immigrants Pranab Chakroborty and Aparna get
united in the foreign territory out of their cultural and linguistic
solidarity. They primarily forge a bond while he comes to the
United States of America to join the *Massachusetts Institute of Technology*. He very often goes to Aparna's house. Usha carries the
tradition as a child addressing Pranab as kaku which means uncle
and he is in turn referring to her mother as 'Boudi' which in Bengali means elder brother's wife. Due to the cultural solidarity, they
feel a pull towards each other which has gradually been trans-

muted into a love relationship. Usha's mother — that is, Boudi — seems to cling to Indian customs wearing sari 'bangle' but she is fond of Pranab Chakroborty which replicates her intimate alienation from her conjugal relationship. Usha being a narrator has aptly described the plight of Aparna, her mother and the crisis in her conjugal relationship:

> My father was a lover of silence and solitude. He had married my mother to placate his parents; they were willing to accept his desertion as long as he had a wife. He was wedded to his work, his research, and he existed in a shell that neither my mother nor I could penetrate. Conversation was a chore for him; it required an effort he preferred to expend at the lab. He disliked excess in anything, voiced no cravings or needs apart from the frugal elements of his daily routine: cereal and tea in the morning, a cup of tea after he got home, and two different vegetable dishes every night with dinner. He did not eat with the reckless appetite of Pranab Kaku. My father has a survivor's mentality. From time to time, he liked to remark, in mixed company and often with no relevant provocation, that starving Russians under Stalin had resorted to eating the glue off the back of their wallpaper. One might think that he would have felt slightly jealous, or at the least suspicious, about the regularity of Pranab Kaku's and the effect they had on my mother's behaviour and mood. But my guess is that my father was grateful to Pranab Kaku for the companionship he provided, freed from the sense of responsibility he must have felt for forcing her to leave India, and relieved, perhaps, to see her happy for change. (ibid. 65-66)

It naturally indicates her utter humiliation and crisis, which pushes her to turn onto Pranab Chakroborty. Aparna's husband is also least bothered about her which gets its resonance:

> Aparna turns so isolated and at times frustrated that she appears to be grudging or complaining soul: When my mother complained to him about how much she hated life in the suburbs and how lonely she felt, he said nothing to placate her. If you are so unhappy, go back to Calcutta,' he would offer, making it clear that their separation would not affect him one way or the other. (ibid. 76)

Moreover, the similarities of the tastes to which both Pranab and Aparna belong seem to unite them in a similar plane. In fact, Aparna who is a staunch practitioner of Indian cultural heritage seems to be deviant while she goes for extramarital relationship with Pranab. On the other hand, initial bonding between Pranab and Usha's family has fallen apart while Pranab makes a departure from this bond by developing intimacy with Deborah, a woman from American culture. Boudi being shocked or enraged says, 'He used to be so different. I don't understand how a person can change so suddenly. It is just hell-heaven, difference." (*ibid*.5). Pranab's decision to marry Deborah generates a tension in the mind of his parents and a jealousy in Aparna too thinking about the impending cultural dissimilarities: "Pranab Kaku's parents were horrified by the thought of their only son marrying an American woman" (*ibid*.68). Deborah, his new American wife though tries to learn certain Bengali words to make a connection with new culture but her life style and dominance over Pranab Babu leads to their separation at the end. Deborah tries her level best to maintain relationship with Pranab's parents and never tries to dissuade him from his own cultural heritage: "she had tried, for years to get Pranab Kaku to reconcile with his parents and that she had also encouraged him to maintain ties with other Bengalis, but he had resisted" (*ibid*.82). In fact, Pranab Chakroborty is caught in a sandwich like condition as he is not showing his constancy in terms of relationship and has cheated both Aprna and Deborah, resulting in their ultimate alienation. On the other hand, Usha being the second generation immigrant, seldom pays attention to Indian cultural heritage rather adheres to the western culture. Usha is quite frank in terms of her sexual relationship connoting American individuality which shows antipathy towards Indian cultural tropes. In the story, it seems that Aparna and Debprah are *interpellated* (Krips 73) into the subject of Pranab who has utilised them and left them according to his whims. This is what is somehow related to the patriarchy and subjugation of womanhood. So, all the characters in this story are psychologically dislocated, though in different parts of their life, they meet different Others which accords Levinisian ethics that meeting the face of the others is of an order which is other than simple and pure perception. In such encounter the 'ego' or 'self' feels responsibility for the others who look at him. Such responsibility for the other is 'incumbent' on the 'self' (Matravers 153). So, the characters engrafted in this story are intimately associated and alienated at the end in different moments of their life which denotes continuous deferral of their selves having no specific axis which is akin to Levinas's concept of 'saying' over the 'said' (Llewellyn 126).

"A choice of Accommodation" denotes a different type of accommodation, far from the madding crowd and spacio-temporal location. Unlike the other parents of Lahiri, Amit's parents are not at all alluded with the memory of their home rather they are willing to move on and on having no destiny. Such nomadic parents can have a resonance in the story:

> His parents, unlike most other Bengalis in Massachusetts, had always been dismissive, even critical of India, never homesick or sentimental. His mother had short hair and wore trousers, putting on saris only for special occasions. His father kept a liquor cabinet and liked a gin and tonic before his meals. They both came from wealthy families, had both summered in hill stations and attended boarding schools in India themselves. The relative affluence of America never impressed them; in many ways they had lived more privileged lives in India, but they left the country and had not looked back. (*Unaccustomed* 96)

They somehow are very much akin to the global transnationalism. Amit did not get any emotional attachment from his mother, which tends to make him acerbic enough. Amit feels absolutely alienated while he goes to Delhi to stay

> in their flat full of servants in Chittaranjan Park... He never enjoyed his visits to Delhi, his broken Bengali of no use in that city. It made him miss Calcutta, where all his relatives lived, where he was used to going. His parents had moved to Delhi the year of Indira Gandhi's assassination, and the riots that subsequently raged there, the curfews and the constant vigilance with which his parents had to live, meant that Amit remained cooped up inside, without friends, without anything to do. (*ibid* 96)

Amit can hardly conform to the Indian customs; he rather wants to make himself more American. Amit does not follow the paths of his father and leaves medical school. Amit and Megan gradually fall in love with each other during their college days and get married. But what appears as a deterrent to their relationship is that Meghan is five years senior to Amit and her backdrop is very normal, which is yet to fulfil the demands of Amit's family. So, at the very inception, they are surreptitiously married to each other dislocating from home and culture as well. But Amit had a crush on Pam which results in broaching problem in sustaining their conjugal relationship with their two children. Pam while married Ryan, sends Amit's invitation via mails. But while Amit gets married to Meghan, Pam connects herself with Amit through occasional mails. Being invited by Pam on the occasion of her marriage, Amit drinks a lot, and is completely oblivious to her wife. He even does not know how she returns to home; even the keys of the car are in his pocket. Both Amit and Meghan had had a plan "[...] we are staying here until tomorrow (ibid.120). He further says, "I am sorry, Meg. The drinks went straight to my head. I don't even remember having that many. I didn't mean to abandon you" (ibid.120). Meghan has really been missing his accompaniment and she has made her ejaculation "I have spent enough time at this weeding by myself" (ibid.21). At the end of the story, both Meg and Amit have made their love outside the room rather in Nature where they are absorbed and merged into each other: "He came inside her and sat up, knowing they could not linger." (ibid.126). Prick of conscience stirs Amit's inner self for not showing his responsibility to Meghan during Pam's marriage ceremony but lastly, "he hoped that he was forgiven, and for a new moments they remained together on the narrow bed in the little room, his heart biting rapidly, vigorously, plainly striking the skin of her palm" (ibid.127). Moreover, the names of Amit's two daughters are Maya and Magan, which sound Indian but being third-generation Indian-Americans, they are completely Americans: "Both Maya and Monika had inherited Megan's colouring, without a trace of Amit's deeply tan skin and black eyes, so that apart from their vaguely Indian names they appeared fully American" (ibid. 94). Hence, the gap which once was generated had gained its fulfillment after his association with Megan with their second child in a new manner. So, change becomes quite important in this connection to solve any problem.

In the story "Only Goodness", Sudha and Rahul, both being second-generation immigrants, desperately seek to exonerate themselves from the clutches of their parental caring. As Lahiri writes, "Sudha's persona scholarly, her social life limited to other demure girls in her class, if only to ensure that one day she would be set free" (*Unaccustomed* 129). She completely adopts western culture by partying, engaging in free love, and drinking — of which her parents are ignorant. She also thinks her parent's attitude as "puritanical, frowning upon the members of their Bengali circle" (*ibid.*129). Sudha also introduces alcohol to Rahul, her brother. Due to their excessive adherence to the Western Culture, they are intimately alienated from Bengali circle or ethnic survival emblematic of their separation from parents, first-generation immigrants. Likely, being the first generation immigrants, parents are to stumble in coping with the host culture especially while they are in Wayland as they "faced a life sentence of being foreign" (*ibid.*138). Sudha though extends her hand to their support as she feels "her parents separation from India as an ailment that ebbed and flowed like a cancer" (*ibid.*138). But Rahul says "No one dragged them here. Baba left India to get rich, and Ma married him because she had nothing else to do" (*ibid.*138). Actually, the first-generation immigrants' arrival to host country and their participation in retaining home culture within host and negotiation with both generates symbolic incarceration, leaving a negative impact on the second generation immigrants which make their life acerbic and confused too. While Sudha's parents are in London, asking for ethnic solidarity by renting two rooms in Balham from a Bengali landlord namely Mr. Pal where Sudha's mother was pregnant with Sudha and "elderly British woman who did not allow children under her roof" (*ibid.*135).This is nicely articulating cultural segregation — during that time Sudha's father considered sending her mother back to India to give birth, until they met Mr. Pal, which is very much akin to the ethnic consciousness epitomising togetherness, but children seem to her as "survivors in strange intolerant seas"(*ibid.* 135). Rahul becomes a problem child, erratic and too much free. He cuts a very sorry figure in College exams while Sudha asks him; he replays "He is floundering" (*ibid.*136). And gradually he is drifting from his aim. Rahul's mode of communication becomes quite vituperative which invariably alienates him from the rest whereas a perfect harmony found in terms of the relationship of their parents.

Both her parents came from humble background; both their grandmothers had given up the gold on their arms to put roofs over their families' heads and food on their plates. This mentality, as tiresome as it sometimes felt, also reassured Sudha, for it was something her parents understood and respected about each other, and she suspected it was the glue that held them together. (*ibid.* 140)

However, being the so-called 'coloured people', they have really been suffering from what Gilroy defines as the 'double consciousness' (x): Lahiri writes, "teased at school for the colour of their skin or for the funny things their mother occasionally put into their lunch boxes, potato carry, sandwich that tinted Wonder bread green." (*Unaccustomed* 143). Food items catered to Sudha and Rahul are tinged with the intention of retaining the ethnic consciousness on the part of the first-generation immigrants which is grotesque to the other students belonging to America, resulting in alienation and depression of the second-generation immigrants.

Sudha gets married to a person Roger who is also alcoholic like her. But Rahul surpasses the barrier. He initially decides to write play, suddenly feels that writing play is stupid. Rahul also hastily gets married to Elena, eight years older than Rahul which his father dissents later as he has nothing. Rahul says his father a 'pathetic snob' (*ibid.*155). Though later on Rahul becomes a line cook at Restaurant. However, it can also be located that their parents return to Kolkata, Rahul gets to know it while he comes to Sudha's home to attend Annaprason of her kid Neel. He asks "are they moving for good?" (*ibid.*155). Sudha replies, "May be" (*ibid.*155), which nicely portrays their parents intimate alienation from the host culture and their disoriented children and lead their life in the accustomed place on their whims. Rahul becomes so distanced from his life, while Sudha and Roger goes to movie by handing the child over Rahul to look after but he leaves the kid in a bath tub and Neel could have died which not only proves Rahul's imbecile nature but also disrupts the faith of the conjugal relationship between Sudha and Roger. Rahul is always absorbed in his own world which is quite elliptical and brings problem or distrust between Sudha and Roger consequently. However, cultural conflict between first-generation vis-à-vis second-generation immigrants seems to exhibit different kinds of alienation where first generation is anchored in building up their ethnic solidarity, retaining sanity in terms of their relationships, on the contrary, the second generation immigrants are severely trying to placate themselves from the clutches of their parental influence, nourishing exorbitant individuality, leading them towards absolute alienation and indeterminacy.

In "Nobody's Business", Sangeeta, a Bengali, smart, single-lady of thirty, is the matter of attraction among the many successful handsome men. Their unwanted encroachment upon her private sphere seems to perturb her own world. She does not call it 'love' (ibid.176) as she believes that, "[t]hese men were not interested in her. They were interested in a mythical creature created by an intricate chain of gossip [...]" (ibid.176). Paul and Heather, who are her housemates to whom she also declares her position: "I have a boyfriend" (ibid.176). In fact, she is absolutely free. However, the person whom she loves a lot is Farouk, having a lot of affairs but has a tremendous quality to convince the women as the way he does with Sang and Deirdre. But his false armour seems to be fallen apart while truth comes to the limelight through telephonic conversation between Paul and Deirdre. It really mortifies Sang a lot; she is shocked and closed the door. This room is indicating her intimate alienation from the world to remould or rejuvenate herself disdaining patrimony. After opening the door, we can engineer a different Sang, who "had changed, into a black top with long tight-fitting sleeves. Her pink raincoat was draped over her arm, her purse hanging over her shoulder. I need a ride" (ibid. 211). Indeed, it appears that she simply retorts to Farouk's attitude being intimately alienated from him and sunk into her own world which is generally no body's business to intervene.

"Once in a life time" is a beautiful story tracing upon the loss, gain and infinite destination between first and second generation immigrants which is exquisitely handled in the hands of an innocent narrator Hema, who puffs up imagination into the entire plot and leads us to the world of origin where the parental ideology involved with the typical Indian customs in the alien shore is swallowing up the voices of second generation immigrants like Hema-Kaushik. As Munos interprets,

> Indeed, not only is Hema as a narrator split into a 'narrated I' and a 'narrating I', but Kaushik as addressee and character is divided into a 'narrated you' that is firmly rooted in the past time of the story and a phantasmal, intangible 'addressed you' that exists only as a projection of the narrator's voice, thus extending its ethereal existence beyond the margins of diegetic time. (5)

Hema gets to know Kaushik from 1974 when she was six and he was nine years old. Kaushik's parents take a decision of departing Cambridge and return to India rejecting their struggle in diaspora, unlike Hema's parents and other Bengalis. Hema becomes retrogressive to find out the roots in Kolkata which is a natural propinquity of a diasporic individual. Lahiri competently vindicates the situation, weather, location, time and social condition in portraying the plot of the story. Her childhood innocence is articulated through her narration which explores the solidarity of two Bengali women; one is Kaushik's mother and other one is Hema's mother:

> Our mothers met when mine was pregnant. She didn't know it yet; she was feeling dizzy and sat down on a bench in a small park. Your mother was perched on a swing, gently swaying back and forth as you soared above her, when she noticed a young Bengali woman in a sari, wearing vermillion in her hair. [...] She told you to get off the swing, and then she and you escorted my mother back home. It was during that walk that your mother suggested that perhaps mine was expecting. (*Unaccustomed*224-25)

Hema also announces further the close proximity between the two families which refer to the past memories.

> They shopped together for groceries and complained about their husbands and cooked together at either our stove or yours, dividing up the dishes for our respective families when they were done. They knitted together, switching projects when one of them got bored. When I was born, your parents were the only friends to visit the hospital. I were fed in your old high chair, pushed along the streets in your old pram. (*ibid.* 224-25)

The loneliness and cultural solidarity which both of the mothers come across in the alien soil, help them to be united but their presence in the U.S.A. and their equal response to the loneliness bolster the friendship between Hema and Kaushik consequently:

> In Calcutta, they would probably have had little occasion to meet. Your
> mother went to a convent school and was the daughter of one of Calcutta's
> most prominent lawyers [...]. My mother's father was a clerk in the General
> Post Office, and she had neither eaten at a table nor sat on a commode be-
> fore coming to America. Those differences were irrelevant in Cambridge,
> where they were both equally alone. (*ibid.* 225)

In fact, the very beginning of the story implies Kaushik's presence
in Hema's life which surpasses the confines of her own consciousness beyond the signs he has left:

> I had seen you before, too many times to count, but a farewell party that
> my family threw for yours, at our house in Inman Squire, is when I began
> to recall your presence in my life. (*ibid.* 223)

While Kaushik's family moves back to India which accentuates
Hema's rumination of him. Their relationship is featured from the
very outset by dissolving the boundaries between absence and
presence, self and other also. During the farewell party Hema has
to put on traditional Indian Pajamas which also pushes her towards Kaushik in terms of cultural affinity. Indeed, Kaushik's
absence is felt and recreated too by Hema through the dress codes
left by Kaushik in her home. Hema says:

> I found these clothes ugly and tried to avoid them, but my mother refused
> to replace them. And so I was forced to wear your sweaters, your rubber
> boots on rainy days. One winter I had to wear your coat, which I hated so
> much that it caused me to hate you as a result. [...] I never got used to hav-
> ing to hook the zipper on the right side, to looking so different from the
> other girls in my class with their puffy pink and purple jackets. [...] I want-
> ed desperately to get rid of [the coat]. I wanted it to be lost. (*ibid.* 226)

It seems to signify the porosity of the boundary between self and
other, suggesting the non-acclimatising nature of diasporic legacy
for Hema as a child. She tries to abandon the coat at the school
bus, but it is the name tag that brings her coat back to her, epitomising their inseparable and inescapable bond which is embedded
in Kaushik's old self.

Lahiri through the narration of Hema seeks to perpetuate the
loss identified by her second-generation fictional characters. They
are disoriented, dislocated and propelled by the transgenerational memories, leading them to authenticate their exist-

ence by re-rooting themselves with their shared past where post memories has a poignant role to play. In fact, reincarnating or reimagining the phantom loss by the second-generation immigrants is tending them to reshape their lost generation which is attuned to collective cultural and traumatic events. As Hirsch writes,

> Postmemory is a powerful form of memory precisely because its connection to its object or source is mediated not through recollection but through an imaginative investment and creation. That is not to say that memory itself is unmediated, but that it is more directly connected to the past. Postmemory characterizes the experiences of those who grow up dominated by narratives that preceded their birth, whose own belated stories are displaced by the stories of the previous generation, shaped by traumatic events that can neither be fully understood nor re-created. (662)

In fact, post memory emphasizes upon the parents' homeland, which basically generates a non-symbolical void in the minds of second generation immigrants like Hema–Kaushik and their subsequent destiny. The loss of motherland and mother of Kaushik is prevalent through the presence of him which retains — in Mishra's terminology, a 'primal wound' (116) — one experiences as an infant, is somehow reflected in the second generation migrant subjectivities. Kaushik's father's arrival in the United States of America after seven and proclaiming his new job is his armour to hush up the secret regarding the demise of his wife Parul. Parul Masi, who is fond of Hema, died of breast-cancer, which Kaushik reveals later on with his close conversation with Hema. However, such 'un- dead presence' (qtd. in Munos 19) of his mother looms large in Hema's room which creates an eerie ambience for her. The death of his mother definitely originates a void or melancholia which needs to be represented through words, identifying mourning which Freud indicates. The second-generation immigrant Hema seems to be performing the job extremely well:

> I followed you along the path you had discovered, and then we parted, neither of us a comfort to the other, you shovelling the driveway. I going inside for a hot shower [...]. Perhaps you believed that I was crying for you, or for your mother, but I was not. I was too young, that day, to feel sorrow or sympathy. I felt only the enormous fear of having a dying woman in our home. I remembered standing beside your mother, both of us topless in the

fitting room where I tried on my first bra, disturbed that I had been in such close proximity to her disease. I was furious that you had told me, and that you had not told me, feeling at once burdened and betrayed, hating you all over again. (*Unaccustomed* 250-51)

However, Kaushik, in his conversation with Hema, says that his mother "had made us promise we'll scatter her ashes into the Atlantic" (*ibid*.249).But Kaushik's rejection of burying her dead mother in American soil signals his anxiety of being completely disconnected from India because he has a secret passion towards India and wants from the core that the last rituals of her dead mother would be performed in India, though at the very beginning in lieu of scattering her mother's ashes into the Atlantic, he wants her mother to be buried in, as Munos says, 'somewhere' (249), resulting in Kaushik's feelings of burden and mixed feelings too. Moreover, as Munos adds, "the absence of the motherland-an absence engendering such an incommensurable sense of loss that it often remains unrepresentable and transforms mourning for the land of origins into endless melancholia" (*ibid*. 17). However, the story harps on the intimacy of the two young people amid the dying of Kaushik's mother. 'Once in a Lifetime' ponders over Hema and Kaushik's alienation towards the end of the narrative; Hema comprehends that neither the rigorous diasporic Indianness which her parents signify nor the westernised spurious Indianness Kaushik's mother implies, can bring any final solution for their ensuing days. In fact, Hema's ambivalent attitude towards Kaushik tends them to be more closed and ossified in terms of their relationship. In fine, "the last line of 'Once in a lifetime' performs a hybrid promise: the promise of alchemizing the encounter with otherness into the possibility of mourning" (*ibid*. 22).

In "Years End", the demise of Kaushik's mother mortifies him tremendously and his father's remarriage with a woman Chitra has added fuel to his aching heart. He feels completely misfit in the room after the replacement of his mother in the guise of Chitra, his new mother who has no resemblance to his dead mother. Even, he has to leave his own room for his two new step sisters Rupa and Piu and is compelled to stay at the guest bedroom. Such circumstances generally lead him towards ennui and alienation within his home and invariably such home transmutes into unhomely or *unheimlich* which is not at all a safe place. Chitra's continuous presence in their room develops his habit of mourning. Always he feels a loss which is being materialised through his mourning. He gets somnolent to look at her usage of their kitchen, used to be utilised by his mother earlier:

> I had no memories of my mother cooking here, but the space still retained her presence more than any other part of the house. The jade and spider plants she had watered were still thriving on the windowsill, the orange-and-white sunburst clock she'd so loved the design of, with its quivering second hand, still marking the time on the wall. (*Unaccustomed*263)

In fact, the constant presence of his stepmother and his father appears to animate a sort of numbness in his mind, but on the other hand, he strives to forge an intimacy with his step sisters on the basis of loss they are also embroiled with after losing their father. However, such absence or loss helps them come close to each other: "like them I had lost a parent and was now being asked to accept a replacement" (*ibid*.272). However, such home becomes a ground of oedipal tension for Kaushik since he is severely possessive about his dead mother and his stepsisters gazing at her mother's old pictures is really intolerable for him:

> My mother wearing a swimsuit by the edge of the pool in our old club in Bombay. My mother sitting with me on her lap on the brown wooden steps of our house in Cambridge. My mother and father standing before I was born in front of a snow-caked hedge. (*ibid*. 286)

His inability to share his mother's intimate pictures with his father creates a gulf between him and his father's new life. And consequently his anger falls upon Rupa and Piu and he cannot put up with the replacement of her mother in the guise of Chitra:

> Well, you've seen it for yourselves, how beautiful my mother was. How much prettier and sophisticated than yours. Your mother is nothing in comparison. Just a servant to wash my father's clothes and cook his meals. That's the only reason she's here, the only reason both of you are here. Now the girls were no longer crying, their shiny black heads staring down at the carpet, not moving, saying nothing in reply. I took the shoebox and the rest of my mother's photographs and left the room. I wanted to remove the pictures of the house, as far as I could. [...] My actions felt spontaneous,

> almost involuntary, propelled by the adrenaline of a state of emergency,
> but I realized that on some level I had been thinking of running away for
> days. (*ibid*. 286-87)

Such outburst of his fume tends him to keep on mourning and regenerate his incapability of going beyond such nausea. Hence, such outburst explicates Kaushik's final distraction from his home, his father in America and becomes nomadic and rootless finally. In fact, the shadow of his mother has been inoculated into the minds of Kaushik and his father in such a way which is related to 'the secrets buried alive of one generation-can be perceived in the unconscious of another. What Abraham identifies as the 'transgenerational phantom' (qtd.in Munos 31) in this respect is a "formation of the unconscious" pointing to the transmission of a 'gap', or 'nescience 'i.e "an unknown unrecognized knowledge" (qtd. in Munos 31), as already mentioned, from the parent's psyche to that of the child. In Abram's words:

> What haunts are not the dead, but the gaps left in us by the secrets of oth-
> ers [...]. The phantom is a formation of the unconscious that has never been
> conscious-for good reason. It passes — in a way yet to be determined-from
> the parent's unconscious into the child's. [...]. In no way can the subject re-
> late to the phantom as his or her own repressed experience. The phantom
> which returns to haunt bears witness to the existence of the dead buried
> within the other. (qtd. in Munos 33)

The profundity of his love towards his mother has come to the fore while he is going close to the Canadian border by bringing the shoebox of photographs of his mother. He could not scatter her photographs there rather put them back in the box which is referring to the symbolic burial of his mother's pictured memory in the unaccustomed earth. In fact, thus the continuous battle between self and M(other) is leading Kaushik towards ultimate infinity at the end.

"Going Ashore" is harping on the accidental reunion of Hema and Kaushik in Rome and adumbrating a possibility of their relationship to be condensed via the rumination of their childhood romance; Hema's "heart did not belong to Navin" (*Unaccustomed* 299) who is a Professor of Physics at Michigan State University, and she is going to marry him conforming to the rituals of arranged marriage but she becomes quite distanced from her insipid conjugal life. Her relationship with Navin completely stands on merely occasional phone calls and emails which are completely devoid of emotion. Hence, she is hankering after freedom by engaging herself in her research-works. As a matter of fact, she goes to Rome as a visiting lectureship at the institute of classical studies where she enjoys her freedom truly:

> Now she was free of both of them, free of her past and free of her future...She was alone with her work, alone abroad for the first time in her life, aware that her solitary existence was about to end. (*ibid*. 298)

She does not even think of taking children and openly enjoys her life with a person Julian whom he loved. She realises "something dead about the marriage she was about to enter into...she was conscious only for its deadness". (*ibid*.301)

However, Kaushik's sudden appearance at Rome as a photo-journalist brings up an opportunity to reawaken their childhood romance with a new vigour in a new place. Kaushik as a photo-journalist goes to war-zones of Israel, Guatemala, Mexico, Africa and Middle East for taking pictures of corpses. His nomadic existence starts from his childhood, he "was happiest to be outside, away from the private detritus of life" (*ibid*.309). After Kaushik's arrival in Rome and his association with Hema leads them to share their intimate relationship after a prolonged gap which seems to make them rejuvenated: "She stayed awake, listening to his breathing, craving his touch" (*ibid*.314). But she thinks of his temporality as he will no longer be there and very soon he is going to Hong Kong and she would go to India. Even, he is utilising condom in their sexual relationship with Hema which is also referring to the invisible wall between them, and it is yet to be mended. So, while Kaushik insists her to cancel her impending marriage with Navin but she replies, "It's too late, Kaushik" (*ibid*.322). In fact, Hema's attachment with Kaushik in Rome is nothing but "the forming of a new community provides a sense of fixity through the language of heritage-a sense of inheriting a collective past by sharing the lack of a home rather than sharing a home" (Ahmed 85).

In fact, Hema actually seeks to re-root herself through the presence of Kaushik. However, her continuous dislocation and relocation in terms of her relationship with Kaushik leads her towards absolute alienation. Hema feels "the one she never removed, the one Kaushik had hooked his finger through the first night, drawing her to him" (*Unaccustomed* 323). But she has left the bangle during the security check in the aircraft. Bangle is the symbol of traditional and cultural heritage which seems to help her to be related to her ancestral home in Rome: "...she felt she had left a piece of her body behind. She had grown up hearing from her mother that losing gold was inauspicious" (*ibid*.324).

Kaushik on the other hand "didn't want to leave it up to chance to find her again, didn't want to share her with another man...without her he was lost" (*ibid*.326). In fact, both of them are living on different shore who happen to meet altogether in a different place with an intensity of passion and emotion, but it provides them temporary pleasure and yields far reaching impulse to both in general but Hema in particular. Hema's madness after having the shocking news of his premature death can be felt in the story: "I felt it as plainly and implacably as the cells that were gathering and shaping themselves in my body. Those cold, dark days I spent in bed, unable to speak, burning with new life but mourning your death" (*ibid*.333). She is frantically searching any traces of Kaushik in websites, but she laments that Kaushik 'had left nothing behind' (*ibid*.333). This story is really denoting the migrant's (that is, Hema's) predicament for being too much individualistic and her dream of survival in the alien soil through the remembered past which Kaushik is encapsulating through his absent presence existence.

In fine, "Unaccustomed Earth", the short story collection, has been discussed from the psychoanalytical vantage point in which the fictional characters are in constant oscillation between the past and the present, and more importantly, they are in a desperate attempt to place themselves in their unaccustomed Earths. It reveals the generational gap among the characters and amalgamation of emotion and culture.

Chapter 3:

Diasporic Subjectivity:
an aporetic journey in *The Namesake*

> The most beneficial contribution of diasporic studies may be its problema-
> tisation of subjectivity. What appears to be the unsettled and unsettling
> space of dislocation, of displacement, or exile, offers, at least potentially,
> the opportunity to discard forever the illusion of fixed identity. Diaspora
> confirms human subjectivity as a function of difference. But difference is
> not just a juxtaposition of identities. Difference is what is happening within
> the very moment bodies and forces cut across each other, merge and sepa-
> rate, transform and change. Difference, like freedom, only has meaning in
> the act of differing. And this act is continual: all difference, in other words,
> lies in the act of differing. The really difficult thing for human subjects to
> comprehend, given their entrapment within the discourse of history, na-
> tion, race, ethnicity, is that all subjectivity is different in its differing. It is
> this that is normal, not the fixity of cultural or national identity, the convic-
> tion of one true, shared, essential being. Yet it is this one true identity that
> acts as the magnetic north to subjectivity, drawing it inexorably into the
> myth of unity, creating immense anxiety upon any deviation from this
> norm. (qtd. in Ashcroft 8).

However, the diasporic individuals obviously stand on various
cultural cross roads, which tend to form in-betweenness where
one can confront with foreignness in the host country, return to
his or her root or can celebrate the both. Lahiri's second novel *The
Namesake* (2003) really upholds the First generation and second
generation immigrants' conditions within the cultural crossroads
and also brings to the fore as to how they challenge the cartographical epistemology, and thereby bringing out the concept of
transnationalism.

The Namesake involves with the travelling of the first-
generation immigrants from home to the host culture in search of
job, economy, which results in the difficulty to cope with the foreign culture not only for them, but likely to the second generation
immigrants. Ashoke Ganguly comes to the United States of America in The Massachusetts University for career and job where
Ashima comes with him for accompaniment. Ashima's dislocation

from her root baffles her a lot, especially while she is pregnant, which leads her to thus reflect:

> ... being a foreigner [...] is a sort of lifelong pregnancy — a perpetual wait, a constant burden, a continuous feeling out of sorts. It is an ongoing responsibility, a parenthesis in what had once been ordinary life, only to discover that the previous life has vanished, replaced by something more complicated and demanding. Like pregnancy, being a foreigner, Ashima believes, is something that elicits the same curiosity from strangers, the same combination of pity and respect. (Namesake49-50)

Hospital is a biological space where one's body is under the surveillance of the hospital authority. In fact, Foucauldian Governmentality always subjugates patient's body, which morphs the body into marginality. Ashima being a pregnant immigrant individual seeks to have accompaniment from the host culture which has a sheer lack. This circumstance makes her retrogressive towards her home culture, which refers to a crowd or togetherness at the time of pregnancy. However, such inertia makes her alienated, but still she is subjugated because of the Governmentality, stemming from the host culture at the hospital where she is fighting on her own with her difficulties. In fact, the ethno-cultural burden she desperately realises in the hostland. Ashima Ganguli suffers from the lack of togetherness or crowd, which she used to experience in India — that is, her home. However, being the first-generation immigrants, Mr and Mrs Ganguli perform their ethnic, cultural rituals at home and their children Gogol and Sonia acclimatise with both the home and abroad; it is conducive to the formation of in-betwenness including their parents also. Ashima alienates herself from her home, and yet she mourns for the lack of absence laid in her unconscious mind. In fact,

> Mourning is regularly the reaction to the loss of a loved person or to the loss of some abstraction which has taken the place of one, such as one's country, liberty, an ideal, and so on. In some people the same influences produce melancholia instead of mourning and we consequently suspect them of a pathological disposition. (Freud 243)

However, she still nourishes a nationalistic fervour within herself by resorting to Partha Chatterjee who:

...draws a distinction between nationalism as a political movement, which challenges the colonial state, and nationalism as a political movement, which challenges the colonial state, and nationalism as a cultural construct, which enables the colonised to posit their difference and autonomy. The former is derivative, but the latter draws its energies from other sources. Chatterjee's argument is that anticolonial nationalism attempts to create "its own domain of sovereignty within colonial society. (Aikant, Satish C 59)

By celebrating her own ethnic culture at home in the host land, she tends to formulate ghetto mentality. In order to materialise the loss of her motherland, she resorts to memory, which delimits any spacio-temporal barrier. Ashima completely dismantles the geo-political aspects of the home being driven by 'homing desire' (Brah 192), which is considering home to be a 'mythic place of desire in diasporic imagination' (*ibid.* 192). In fact, after the demise of her husband, she gets tremendously shocked: "For the first time in her life, Ashima has no desire to escape to Calcutta" (*Namesake* 183). She starts to live in her home for six months and also longs to stay in the host country for six months, which really transmutes her character into transnational or borderless. She herself proclaims after the birth of Gogol "I'm saying I don't want to raise Gogol alone in this country. It's not right. I want to go back" (*ibid.*33). Such mentality of Ashima connotes the diasporic predicament Ashima is trapped into. Ashima initially dislocates herself with her husband from home to the host culture where she celebrates her home culture and after returning to her home, she longs for the host culture, which proves her intention to get herself truncated from any specific space-time continuum, and thereby seeking to anticipate her alienation intimately beyond the continents; her name testifies to such attitude positively.

However, *The Namesake*, which is set in the foreign territory, is a beautiful delineation of an immigrant family, negotiating with the new socio cultural milieu. The members of the family mature up 'American'. It is initially a story of second-generation immigrant Gogol or Nikhil who is straddling between two oppositional cultural milieus, which splits his identity and broaches profound sense of uncertainty in him. He assumes the condition of A.B.C.D (American Born Confused Desi). Gogol, Sonia, Moushumi, the second generation immigrants, become also the victim of such cross-cultural atmosphere, which indicates to be or not to be condition for them. Much of Gogol's tension crops up from his name—Gogol. In fact, the influence of Russian literature is resonated in the nineteenth-century Babu Culture. Ashok Ganguli is a part of such culture, having insurmountable interest in Russian Literature, which provokes him to give his son's name Gogol. This name is very special for Ashoke Ganguli as it was associated with the train accident while he was reading the book of Nikolai Gogol's *Overcoat*. Indeed,

> Throughout the twentieth, there has been a long-standing relationship between Indians and Russian literature, and particularly between Bengal and Russia. For most of the years since its formation in 1964, the government of West Bengal has been ruled by CPI (M)—the communist party of India (Marxist), which aligned itself with the Soviets. (qtd. in Dhingra and Cheung 39)

In the 1966-article entitled "Russian Studies in India", A.R. Chakraborty argues in favour of expanding the Russian curriculum in post-British India, both as a counterpoint to the British influence, and to train interpreters and translators due to the growing economic and cultural relations with the Soviet Union, and perhaps, as the new nation tried to form alliances with another major power. He argues that historically Russian literature was studied in India:

> ...not so much for its literary value as for its political implications'. Although he does not mention Gogol, he states that "some of the greatest Russian writers (for example, Tolstoy, Turgenev, and Gorky) were translated into Indian languages'. At the height of the cold war, the Bengali scholar argued in favour of the Ministry of Education's establishing the Indian Institute of Russian Studies and Russian departments in Universities. (qtd.in Dhingra and Cheung 39)

Russian literature yields a postcolonial legacy which is neither American nor British, rather represents an alternative tradition. Lahiri seems to lead us to imagine a completely different world bereft of typical British, American, or even Indian context. In fact, it indicates a kind of neo-colonialism, which is reflected through Ashoke's behaviour and the act of naming. Bengali title 'Gangopadhya', dissolves into 'Ganguli', is also an example of Anglicization, reminding us the Spivakian concept of 'catachresis'. Apropos to 'catachresis', Spivak proclaims:

> The catachresis involved in original Indian nation' is not just that there is no one 'tribe' including all aboriginals resident in what is now 'India'. It is also that the concept 'India' is itself not 'Indian', and further, not; identical with the concept *Bharata*, just as nation and jati have different histories. Furthermore, the sentiment of an entire nation as place of origin is not a statement within aboriginal discursive formations, where locality is of much greater importance. (141)

In fact, the concept of naming and named is steeped in colonial ideology, having a recurrent motif to represent colonised according to their convenience. 'Nilanjana Sudeshna Lahiri' has been shortened by and into 'Jhumpa Lahiri'; similarly, 'Gangopadhyay' has been transmuted into 'Ganguli'. The same issue is related to the incident of selecting the name of 'Gogol'. In fact, in the South-Asian context in particular, catachresis is coupled with modernity at the moment of colonial encounter and this plays into *The Namesake*. Cutting himself from his own cultural roots, Ashok develops intimacy with the host culture, which galvanises his root. But at home, he also practises his own ethno-cultural tools, too, but such buffer zone in which he resides at present reveals his inability to forge any equipoise in terms of cultural syncretism. Gogol feels this name to be incongruous with his socio-cultural self. Hence, he alters it into Nikhil ("he who is entire, encompassing all" (*Namesake* 56). I would like to entitle the novel 'Nameshakes' in lieu of 'Namesakes' as Gogol has to go through a lot of consternations regarding his naming where he has to battle with the indigenousness and the Western-ness on a daily-basis, which really places him in a contingent zone, connoting the ambiguity of his existence. Gogol, who gradually evolves as an empowered individual, is caught in cultural pluralism and develops the idea of the *third space*. In fact, third-space is a transnational space in which identities are plural and fluid, and Gogol, by changing his name to 'Nikhil', conforms to that space. Gogol and Sonia are completely drifting themselves from their moral baggages tied to their ancestral culture; they are also engaged in lots of individual affairs, which bring no sanity in life, and it articulates their adherence to the epicurean western culture. The penultimate result brings out nothingness, cultural shock. In fact, Gogol's marriage to Moushumi by emulating the solemnized marital procedure seldom shows happy ending because they are completely engrossed in the foreign culture, and they are unwilling to go through ethnic consciousness as catered by their parents. Excessive freedom, avoidance of rules, and intimacy with the foreign culture perceptively act as a deterrent to the progression of their relationship. Since, Marriage is the institution, it seeks to unite Gogol and Moushumi on the corporeal ground, but they are discarded mentally. Intimacy with solidarity, which is the replica of Indian culture, is perpetuated by Ashima at the outset of the novel. Such phenomenon is gradually replaced by the intimacy with individuality as portrayed through the character of Gogol and Moushami (second-generation immigrants); they represent segregation or continuous deferral of homogeneity. 'Moushami', a name in the Indian context, denotes 'undecidibility', and their marital destination is also steeped in aporia. In fact, the ultimate destination of the second generation immigrants in the diaspora is aporetic, and the constitution of their individual self is being generated through the dialectic and difference.

The Namesake is replete with so many immigrant individuals, who are interacting with each other, having the various strands of cultures. These are conducive to the formation of the diasporic individuals. This is referring to the unification of immigrant folk within a specific space called family. Family in a diasporic context is a space felt generally through the web of relations. Family assumes a kind of space in the immigrant location where cultural, rituals, religious rites are performed by a community to retain ethnic cultural values of one's own. The existence of familial space is dependent on the continuous iteration and performances of the 'lived body' belonging to the ethnic group in the host country, and thereby, trying to keep their cultures alive in the United States of America. Family becomes a site of contestation between keeping one's own ancestral culture and adopting with the host culture. Such pressure, which is stemming from both the roots and routes, seems to generate a cultural lag, and it is mostly overt in the portrayal of the second generation immigrants, who are simply unable to maintain the pressure of the different cultural milieus. In fact, the second-generation immigrants, who seem to represent the impossibility of a permanent return, are straddling between 'here' and 'there', which is termed as "vacuum culture" (qtd.in Mishra 184) by Gauri Bhat. Ashoke and Ashima lived in two different family spaces in India. Marriage being a social institution unites them together. They now forge a family related to the network of kith and kin. They are now conforming to the form of 'model minority' through the process of kinship network. It was the age of 1968 while telephone and internet connection were about to reach-helped them keep in touch with the kith and kins in India. In fact, Ashoke and Ashima, who belong to the first generation immigrants, develop themselves in the United States of America, and the family has been expanded with the birth of their off springs Gogol and Sonia. Apropos to Gogol, it is being said,

> Gogol, an indistinct blanketed mass, reposing in his weary mother's arms. She stands on the steps of the hospital, staring at the camera, her eyes squinting into the Sun. Her husband looks on from one side, his wife's suitcase in his hand, smiling with his head lowered. Gogol enters the World", his father will eventually write on the back in Bengali letters. (*Namesake* 29)

While they arrived at 'home', they were 'suddenly a family' (*ibid*. 32). With the birth of Sonia, it also became an entire family. After the demise of Ashoke, Ashima is unable to abject America, rather she splits her time between her ancestral homes and adopted home. Gogol becomes much closer to his family after the death of his father.

Arjun Appadurai exhibits locality as "primarily relational and contextual rather than scalar or spatial" (178). He develops the sense of locality against the term 'neighborhood' which, according to him, denotes:

> ... the actually existing social forms in which locality, as a dimension of value, is variably realised ...Neighbourhoods, in this usage, are situated communities characterised by their actuality, whether spatial or virtual, and their potential for social reproduction. (*ibid*.179)

Locality is "a complex phenomenological quality, constituted by a series of links between the sense of social immediacy, the technologies of interactivity, and the relativity of contexts. This phenomenological quality, which expresses itself in certain kinds of agency, sociality, and reproducibility, is the main predicate of locality as a category (or subject) [...]" (ibid. 178). Locality is a space coupled with certain rites and rituals containing social values, which can be reproduced in the appropriate contexts. In fact, the production of the 'local subject', who are 'actors' belonging to "a situated community of kin, neighbours, friends and enemies" (ibid. 179). He observes:

> Ceremonies of naming and tonsure, scarification and segregation, circumcision and deprivation are complex social techniques for the inscription of locality onto bodies. Looked at slightly differently, they are ways to embody locality as well as to locate bodies in socially and spatially defined communities [....]. Such rites are not simply mechanical techniques for social aggregation but social techniques for the production of 'natives[...]. (ibid.179)

Locality, which carries social values, is performed by the individuals, and thus entering into the concept of 'lived body'. In fact, the absorption of the locality into the lived bodies is socially, culturally constructed which indicates community. In fact, the individuals' performances outside the spatially situated neighbourhood are tending them to generate their distinct existence within the host country. Cultural disparity might be the hindrance emanating from the host culture in sustaining one's own ethno-cultural identity, but performing rituals, food items, rites are nothing but reinforcing locality a lot. In fact, throughout the entire process, it may cause difference of subject from those, who are firmly situated in the neighbourhood of the new space. Locality is an abstract space where cultural traits are carried forward and a compact negotiation is usually built up between the members in the family and the community. It is a space where affection and hate are built up; attraction and repulsion are in allotropic condition, and where rites and rituals are shown to forge a family and community building. The bodies of the members contain the signals prescribed by the particular community to which family belongs. In fact, the ceremonies create local bodies in the foreign territory and seek to tinker a bond with the situated communities. In this way, natives are produced in the diasporic space. Turning aside from the norms creates a kind of tension and uncertainty in the family. In the family while the children get married in different communities, they are considered to be the annihilators of the social and religious cults as inculcated by the family. They are deemed to be nonconformists in emulating social immediacy in the diasporic space, which results in degradation of familial relationship and especially a wide chasm generated between the first generation and the second generation immigrants. The border of locality is actually very porous and open to invasion of foreign rules and rituals. In fact, such invasion is inevitable and it foregrounds the tension among the family situated in the host country. Natives are produced basically in the diasporic space by dint of following the rites and rituals, which help them retain their ethnic culture. Ashima and Ashoke Ganguli, the first generation of immigrants, put emphasis on their ethno-cultural slabs at home, which genuinely refer to a continuum of Bengali community, they are uprooted from their home due to their career purpose. In fact, the production of the diasporic subject is made through their continuous oscillation between the home and the host culture. Lahiri in *The Namesake* seeks to exhibit the marriage ceremony of Ashoke and Ashima, which occurred in India, and they conformed to the rites and rituals of the Bengali community. This apparently seems to be incongruous to the non-westerns:

> She (Ashima) was seated on a piri that her father had decorated, hoisted five feet off the ground, carried out to meet the groom. She had hidden her face with a heart-shaped betel leaf, kept her head bent low until she had circled him seven times. (*Namesake* 10)

The annaprasana or first-rice ceremony in the Cambridge house of the Gangulis also refers to the strategic essentialism of Bengali community as portrayed by Lahiri, which yields a distinct position to the Bengalis living in the foreign country.

> A handful of women ululateas the proceedings begin. A conch shell is repeatedly tapped and passed around, but no one in the room is able to get it

> to emit a sound. Blades of grass and a Pradeep's slim, steady flame are
> held to Gogol's head. (*ibid*.40)

Women are expert in the practice of ululation and blowing the
conch shell, too, in the United States of America. According to
Bengali customs, the maternal uncles usually perform the rituals
and preside over the programme. However, although Gogol's
uncle remains absent in the United States, his role is performed by
Dilip Nandy, a Bengali friend of the Gangulis. All efforts have
been given to reinforce the rituals in the United States of America.
This confirms a ground of producing hybrid culture wherein inherent and acquired culture are intermeshing together, and the
native cultural slabs, which are performed over there, demand
improvisation:

> To predict his future path in life, Gogol is offered a plate holding a clump
> of cold Cambridge soil dug up from the backyard, a ballpoint pen, a dollar
> bill, to see if he will be a landowner, scholar, or businessman. (*ibid*. 40)

Bengali cultural trend of annaprasana is performed in a very apt
way, but the future generation of the children belonging to the
second-generation and third-generation might follow it, or might
adhere to the American ceremonial process. Gogol and Sonia,
being second-generation immigrants, are prone to concentrate
more on the American cultural values, and thus bringing in difficulties in identity building.

In *The Namesake*, food also becomes a metaphor for accentuating cultural values associated both with the home and the host
culture. Gogol's interest in non-Indian food items is naturally
connoting his cultural location of different mould, which clashes
with his parents, who are fond of *desi* types of food items attuned
to their ancestral culture. Anita Mannur broaches the term "culinary citizenship" to mean "that which grants subjects the ability to
articulate national identity via food" (Mannur 20). However, "culinary citizenship" of Ashoke and Ashima in this connection is
definitely Indian. Their food habits and their desire for particular
food item lead them towards their inherent culture. They are le-
gally American citizens, but mentally they are in elsewhere—

belonging to their own home culture. Mannur believes that "culinary narratives which are embedded with nostalgia, control immigrant memories and affect an imagined return to the 'homeland'" (ibid. 27). In The Namesake, there is a beautiful delineation of jhalmuri (though the name has not been mentioned in the text) being prepared by Ashima during her pregnancy.

> on a sticky August evening two weeks before her due date, Ashima Ganguli stands in the Kitchen of a Central Squire apartment, combining Rice Krispies and Planters peanuts and chopped red onion in a bowl. She adds salt, lemon juice, thin slices of green chilli pepper, wishing there were mustard oil to pour into the mix. (Namesake 1)

In an attempt to reproduce jhalmuri in the host country, they seem to bring out their ties with their home culture, and thereby trying to relive their ethnic culture through such practices: "the snack sold for pennies on Calcutta sidewalks and on railway platforms throughout India, spilling from newspaper cones" (ibid.1).

Though the Gangulis seek to materialise the typical Indian food tradition in the host territory, but they feel a definite lack here: "there is something missing" (ibid. 1). They are adjusting in the new circumstances also. Though Ashima and Ashoke are stick to their ethnic food items, they allow their children to have hybrid food ways also. They, in fact, offer no resistance in this connection.

> In the supermarket they [the parents] let Gogol fill the cart with items that he and Sonia, but not they, consume: individually wrapped slices of cheese, mayonnaise, tuna fish, and hot dogs. For Gogol's lunches they stand at the deli to buy cold cuts, and in the mornings Ashima makes sandwiches with bologna or roast beef. At his insistence, she concedes and makes him an American dinner once a week as a treat, Shake'n Bake chicken or Hamburger prepared with ground lamb. (ibid. 65)

Gogol and his compatriots, all second-generation Indian Americans, are, to use Mannur's phrase, "harbingers of new form of cosmopolitanism" (ibid. 22) or even "a new form of racial fusion" (ibid. 22). The new culinary culture that is often celebrated as the first "postnational cuisine" — the 'fusion cuisine' — befits the new generation." (ibid. 22). Gogol's food habit is a truly 'postnational' one which is overt in a neutral space like an airport or aeroplane in flight.

The members of the second-generation have, in Arjun Appadurai's phrase, 'nostalgia without memory' (30). In fact, the family becomes a site for contestation of cultural values to the members of second-generation immigrants. Family is inhabited by an intense politics of memory. However, Gogol, Sonia and Mousumi live in 'a post nostalgic phase' (ibid.31). Ashok and Ashima's visit to their ancestral land is reinforcing their strong adherence to the old cultural moorings, which seem to retard the post-industrial, post-nostalgic time. Gogol suffers from anxiety and trauma emanating from his engagement both in the American and Indian time and space. Being deported from her home country, Ashima feels the same like that of Gogol, but she is more attached to her home culture. Lahiri is exquisitely delineating kinship structure in the novel:

> Gogol and Sonia must remember to say, not aunt this and uncle that but terms much more specific: mashi and pishi, mama and maima, kaku and jethu to signify whether they are related on their mother's or their father's side, by marriage or by blood. (Namesake 81)

While Gogol and Sonia were in Kolkata, they feel uncomfortable to cope with that culture and had to go through the difficult time there: "Gogol never thinks of India as Desh. He thinks of it as Americans do, as India" (ibid.118). This confirms his cultural disparity with his parents. Examining the trends of recent diaspora, Natalie Friedman states that immigrants and their children are no longer 'locally tied' (113). They are now part of what Arjun Appadurai deems the world of 'global flows' (ibid.113). Friedman also suggests that tourism "becomes a useful way of examining the psychic condition of the cosmopolitan children of immigrants in Lahiri's novel" (115). Her interpretation of Gogol as a tourist is also worthy of consideration:

> In an act that mirrors Ashima's decision to divide her time between her two home countries, Gogol returns to her parents' house in Cambridge for a farewell Christmas celebration-the narrator implies, at this point, that Gogol has been dividing his time between New York, his adopted home,

and Cambridge, his parental home, but that with Ashima's retirement to India, Gogol will be, effectively without a home. His return is figured out as a homecoming as much as recognition that he has indeed never left his home and that in his adult life he must encounter the unsettled and un-fixed feeling that his parents felt on their arrival in America. (*Namesake* 123)

On the other hand, Moushumi does not have any problem to stay in the United States and European countries. She is quite cosmo-politan in nature. Her preference for 'third language' and 'third culture' is helping her being a tourist to negotiate with the world.

However, diasporic individuals, who face difficulties within the foreign territory due to their close association with their roots, perpetuate their loss by performing their ancestral cultural mech-anisms. This refers to a kind of escapism of the diasporic individ-uals from the host culture, they are considered as 'forever foreign-er'. Alfred Adler in fact states that "individuals as social beings with free will power can acclimatise with loss by exercising direct-ly or indirectly strategies of compensation." (qtd. in Dhingra and Cheung 29). Behaving like that of American by learning English language cannot make oneself American in the true sense of the term, rather to put in Adler's word, one needs to thrive one's own potential or 'will power' to sustain in the foreign realm, indeed. In fact, the first generation immigrants Ashoke and Ashima seem to generate an ethnic enclave by clinging to their ancestral cultural heritage, thereby seeking to have solidarity in the host culture. In contrast, Gogol and Sonia are identifiably confused individuals as they are practising their paternal cultures at home and performing their inherent American culture outside the room. A kind of dia-logic impact can be found because Gogol seems to feel quite acer-bic in following paternal Indian culture, and is quite potent in emulating American culture. But after the demise of his father, Gogol is obsessed with the name 'Nikhil' which indicates division within his own individuality. Hence, the second-generation immi-grants like Gogol, Moushumi, and Sonia remain distanced from the Indian culture, and they are quite erratic and individualistic in their decisions, which fall them into the abyss. In fact, major char-acters in this novel live inside a set of relations and communicate with spaces of various types, and thereby rendering mobility to

Lahiri's fictional characters. Hence, the space becomes invariably heterogeneous in terms of engagement of diasporic individuals in the different contexts. Indeed,

> The space in which we live, which draws us out of ourselves, in which the erosion of our lives, our time and our history occurs, the space that claws and gnaws at us, is also, in itself, a heterogeneous space. In other words, we do not live in a kind of void, inside of which we could place individuals and things. We do not live inside a void that could be coloured with diverse shades of light, we live inside a set of relations that delineates sites which are irreducible to one another and absolutely not superimposable on one another. (qtd. in Lahiri 2)

This has a vehement reference to the formation of diasporic individuals, in this novel, which are being constituted through the dialectic and difference. In fact, diasporic subjectivity within the cultural crossroads is being constituted through the act of differing. However, such act of differing among the first and second generation immigrants varies in different locations and places, tending them to anticipate their individual aporetic journey.

Chapter 4:

Dialectic and differences: Towards a new cultural identity in *The Lowland*

Homi Bhabha in his *The Location of Culture* (1994) denotes:

> the in-between spaces as terrains for elaborating strategies of selfhood-singular or communal that initiate new signs of identity, and innovative sites of collaboration, and contestation, in the act of defining the idea of society itself...It is in the emergence of the interstices-the overlap and displacement of domains of difference-that the intersubjectivity and collective experiences of nationness, community interest, or cultural value are negotiated. (2)

As diasporic people settle and start their lives in the foreign countries, their home culture gradually get changed. The host culture is hegemonic, having a dominance upon the home culture, which embarks upon the assimilation of the home with the host culture. This is what generates the in-between spaces. Hence, diasporic lived culture is to some extent different from the traditional practices inherent in the 'home culture'. This lived culture can be compared with Raymond Williams' assessment of culture in *Culture and Society* (1985) where he says that "Culture is a record of our reactions in thought and feeling, to the changed conditions of our common life" (285). In fact, the diasporic lived body is dependent on the performances of the individuals, which keep on changing within the crosscurrent of the home visa-vis the host cultural dialectic. Each and every diasporic character is yet to be confined to any specific horizon, so, they create their identities through the transformation and difference. The word 'horizon' is derived from a Greek verb meaning 'to circumscribe'. It became a key concept in phenomenology when it first appeared in Husserl's *Ideas* (1913), referring to the circumference in which all things, real and imaginable are bound to appear spread out in space endlessly, and in time becoming and become, without end. In Husserl the horizon is the principle by which both meaning and its open possibilities appear to us. While the boundary remains central to western epistemology, the horizon, with its merging of location and possibility, renders boundaries problematic. Horizon, the ultimate oculercentric metaphor, throws the spatial boundaries of "Western epistemology itself into doubt. The function of horizon in postcolonial studies lies in its engagement with conceptual boundaries as well as the boundaries of meaning...Throughout the world, formal modes of organization, institutions, metaphorically bounded sites, are traversed by informal spaces, inhabited by diasporas, migrants, exiles, refugees, nomads. These are sites of what might be called interstitial emergence but it is an emergence that functions by means of the act of habitation, through which identity construction takes place (Ashcroft 82).

Jhumpa Lahiri, the winner of Pulitzer Prize for her novel *The Lowland* (2013), depicts her fictional characters under the soft veneer of Naxalite Movement, and seeks to explore the diasporic loss, gain and destination faced by her fictional characters in order to topple the very foundation of the cartographical epistemology. So, she places them in the postcolonial horizons, connoting alterity and possibilities. In fact, due to the transcultural encounter, home becomes a porous object, which becomes more performative by dint of the imaginative fiat of the immigrants; thus, it challenges the geo-political barrier.

Avtar Brah in her book *Cartographies of Diaspora* (2005) defines home as a kind of 'mythic desire' and also wards her fictional characters off any kind of nation-state ideology. *The Lowland* is a brilliant novel entrenched in the backdrop of the Naxalite Movement of 1969. Although, Lahiri is neither engaged in the movement, nor associated with the place Naxalbari, which is situated in the Darjeeling District. The story develops a metahistory wherein love, loss, conflict, alienation are predominant elements. Naxalite Movement in *The Lowland* is adumbrating a new vista of the emergent culture that seeks to impede dominant culture or the state-power, though it fails at the end. Naxalite movement is one of the vital socio political movements occurred in Post-Independence India. The epicenter of this movement is at Naxalbari in May 1967 which is located in the state of West Bengal. This is in fact a peasant movement led by equipped communist revolutionaries who, two years later were to form a party–the CPI (M-L) or the communist party of India (Marxist Leninist), ideologically a part of Maoism. Under the chastisement of Charu Mazumdar, a communist of 49 years of age, they unfurled their voices via peasant revolution or agrarian revolution. The effusion of their movement is to abolish the feudal system which subsumed their voices down the ages. The strategy of guerrilla conflict is deployed by the peasants to exempt from the landlords. Kolkata becomes the centre of Naxalite urban violence from the threshold of the 1970s, targeting police personnel and political rivals. Standing on the era of globalization, Lahiri broaches Naxalite movement to yield a colour to her fictional characters', which is akin to the emergent culture. However, Udayan and Subhas are two intimate brothers as Udayan says "You are the other side of me, Subhas" (*The Lowland* 31). But, they are different in terms of their ideology. Udayan is actively dabbled in the Naxalbari Movement and sacrificed his life for the sake of it at the hands of police. Udayan is pondering over the revolution or the greater self ('boro ami'or 'mature I' in Tagorian sense), on the other hand, Subhas is planning to go abroad for higher studies as he does not want to follow revolution, and is completely mired in his own self ('choto ami'or 'Immature I' in Tagorian sense). They are intimately alienated from each other on the ground of ideology and anticipate their own freedom by dwelling upon their individual world.

Subhas's continuous persistence in carrying forward the Naxalite movement is nothing but a kind of resistance, rendering challenge to the dominant culture entwined with the postcolonial fervour. This confirms his own choice of not being regulated or mapped by the ongoing state hegemony. Now after the pathetic demise of Udayan, there is a sheer loss which revolves round as a spirit and haunts the characters throughout the entire corpus of the novel. His martyrdom is yet to be pacified and invariably reflected in his wife Gauri, who is too bereaved to marry anybody, and she follows the Hindu rituals and wears 'sada-than'. She is totally alienated and becomes intimate with her own world wherein physical Gauri and spiritual Udayan coalesce together. Indeed, the loss, which is very much embedded in her subconscious, helps her revisit her former territory in spite of being separated physically from her Udayan and her place. This actually refers to a *third space* in which she is dwelling independently, having no physical boundaries. She proves any kind of physical boundaries to be false by resorting to imagination. So, she truly conforms to Ashcroft's concept of 'postcolonial horizontalty'. After arriving at home from the host country, Subhas retrieves Gauri from the clutches of the worn-out tradition by marrying her, despite her pregnancy. It generates a combat between the tradition and modernity. Though Gauri initially denies going to the abroad, but Subhas is able to convince her. However, Gauri finally moves to the abroad, but still carries her remembered past. Throughout the entire story, the resonance of Udayan as a spirit is predominant, though Subhas tries his best to give his accompaniment to Gauri. In fact, the continuous presence of Udayan in the mind of Gauri is nothing but referring to the history of Naxalite movement which can be related to Derrida's concept of 'spectralization'. 'Spectralization' is the incarnation of autonomized spirit in an a-physical body that is then taken on as the real body of the living subject:

> The spectre is of the spirit; it participates in the latter and seems from it even as it follows it as its ghostly double.... The production of the ghost, the constitution of the ghost effect is not simply spiritualization or even an autonomization of spirit, idea or thought, as happens par excellence in Hegelian idealism. No, once this autonomization is effected, with the corresponding expropriation or alienation, and only then, the ghostly moment comes upon it, adds to it a supplementary dimension, one more simulacrum, alienation, or expropriation. Namely, a body! In the flesh (leib)! For there is no ghost, there is never any becoming-specter of the spirit without at least an appearance of flesh, in a space of invisible visibility, like the disappearing of an apparition. For there to be ghost, there must be a return to the body, but to a body that is more abstract than ever. The spectrogenic process corresponds therefore to a paradoxical incorporation. Once ideas or thoughts (Gedanke) are detached from their substratum, one engenders some ghost by giving them a body. Not by returning to the living body from which ideas and thoughts have been torn loose, but by incarnating the latter in another art factual body, a prosthetic body, a ghost of spirit. (Cheah 385)

In fact, such a-physical body is reflected in the novel repeatedly through the character of the dead Udayan, emblematic of Naxalite movement of 70s as a spirit.

However, while Gauri places her feet in the United States of America, she becomes very much absorbed in her Ph.D. and studies, which invariably creates a rift within her family space as she is intimately associated with her own world by dissociating herself from her daughter Bela, who is usually looked after by Deepa and Subhas, her father. It indicates her complete leap from the Home to the World that testifies to a NeoIndian womanhood, having a recurrent motif to subvert the so-called Indian sensibility of womanhood which is mired in the very thought of patriarchy, and thereby helping women liberate from their insular lived existence. Concomitantly, they embrace the independent sensibilities looming large in the host culture. Gauri being driven by the free spirit of the host culture, forgets everything to fulfil her desire: "She had California to swallow her; she had wanted to disappear" (*The Lowland* 233). Partha Chateerjee argues in his *The Nation and Its Fragments*,

> The Home was the principle site for expressing the spiritual quality of the national culture, and women must take the main responsibility for protecting and nurturing this quality. No matter what the changes in the external conditions of life for women, they must not lose their essentially spiritual virtues; they must not, in other words, become essentially Westernized. (130)

Gauri fails to perpetuate her spiritual virtues by imbibing western sensibilities in her mind. South Asian Diasporic women characters are really under pressure as their individuality is being constituted by the hegemonic host culture, which offers certain cultural tools to follow up. But Lahirivian heroines pay a deaf ear to this sort of pressure. Lahiri, rather, exonerates her heroines from the discursive nationalism and any specific geographical location and time by imbibing memory that disrupts the fictional border, and thus makes her characters' transnational or borderless (e.g. Ashima in Bengali means borderless). This is called "global flow of culture" (Gikandi 619) and this has been inoculated into the characters of Lahiri, which deconstructs the chronology of the master narrative of Euro American culture. Lahiri proclaims herself to be non extremist in representing any particular cultural strand, having a close rapport with the Tagorean principle of cultural assimilation. However, Chitra Benarjee Divakaruni represents her women characters in her *Arranged Marriage* (1995) her short story collections, and in her novel *The Mistress of Spices* (1997) in such a way, which refer to the domination of the patriarchal society. Bharati Mukherjee makes a negative portrayal of the Indigenous culture by placing herself in the United States of America. But Lahiri retains a disinterestedness towards two cultures which places her characters in flux.

Simon de Beauvoir in her *Second Sex* (1949) projects the feminine aspects of the womanhood, which indicates the submission of the female to the will of the male folk, and it is conducive to the formation of weaker sex or second sex. But, with the passages of time, women dismantle this phallogocentric representation of the society by generating their own niche in which they can go as they wish. Jhumpa Lahiri, the South Asian Diasporic writer, conforms to the conventional gender orientation. Her 'Sexy', *The Namesake*, 'A Temporary Matter' encapsulate the freedom of the second-generation women immigrants by choosing their male partners and thus she justifies heteronormative love affairs. But in her recent novel *The Lowland*, she, for the first time, deviates from this heteronormative love affair, and gives a new vista to probe into it. In fact, the traditional motherhood, which is overt in *The Namesake* through the character of Ashima, can also be found in Subhas's mother Bijoli in *The Lowland*. The staunch rules of the conventional Hindu Pratha, are imposed on Gauri, Udayan's wife, after the demise of her husband, but Subhas defies such worn-out Hindu tradition encoded in the patriarchy and gets married to Gauri, and finally moves to the abroad with her to start their life anew. He, thus, emancipates her from the conventional norms embedded in the ancient Indian Hindu tradition, which clearly refers to a kind of battle prevalent between the tradition and modernity. The emancipation of woman comes to the fore at the hand of Subhas. Though Gauri stays in the Rhode Island, she retains the memory of her former husband Udayan, who was died of the Naxalite movement and it haunts her. Udayan becomes predominant in her life through her prospective baby, Bela, the gift of Udayan, who saw the ray of life in the abroad. Gauri gets married to Subhas only to pursue her study and career, but she cannot resist herself remembering the memory of Udayan, which appears as Freudian 'Uncanny'. So, Udayan becomes a kind of absent presence existence to her and makes her life difficult. She nourishes affliction at the core of her heart, and her constant attempt to negotiate with the foreign culture makes her life more distanced from her child and Subhas. Though, Lahiri's sympathy is always with the male folks since her *Interpreter of Maladies* in which the narrator is male, and her male characters are, in the foreign country, well educated and economically sound (For example, Shukumar is an Indo American doctoral student in "A Temporary Matter", Sanjeev is an Indian American Computer engineer in 'The Blessed House', the Unnamed narrator of "The Third And Final Continent" is A Librarian in the M.I.T., and so on). In fact, Lahiri's male characters are set against the depoliticized backdrop excepting *The Lowland* (composed with the Naxalite Movement). In *The Lowland*, I feel that Lahiri nicely exhibits the tolerance, forbearance, fatherliness, and self sacrifice of Subhas. In spite of being aware of Gauri's cold attitude towards him and Bela, Subhas tries his level best to negotiate with her, and brings up Bela like his own progeny — all these performances, undoubtedly, are the markers of responsibilities that validate Subhas's existence as a father. Lahiri is unusual in her portrayal of Asian American masculinity unlike other South Asian Women writers such as Bharati Mukherjee, Chitra Benerjee Divakaruni and Ginu Kamani. Jhumpa Lahiri moves beyond the identity politics of gender, and does not solely focus on either the female protagonist, or female readers. In fact, the mechanical aspects of the American society swallow her and she is temporarily engaged in same-sex-affair with Lorna:

> Gauri stood up from her desk and shut the door, locking it, knowingly it should have remained open. When she turned around Lorna was facing her, looking at her, standing too close. She took Gauri's hand, putting it inside her T-shirt, on top of her breasts, beneath the pliant material for her

> bra. Gauri felt the nipple under the bra thickening, hardening, as her own were. The softness of the kisses was new. The smell of her, the sculptural plainness of her body as the clothes was removed, as piles of papers were pushed aside to make room on the daybed behind the desk. The smoothness of her skin, the focused distribution of hair. The sensation of Lorna's mouth on her groan. (*The Lowland* 239)

This is actually connoting a new vista, which Lahiri invokes for the first time and thereby pleading for alternative identity through her fictional character Gauri. Thus, she matures herself up as an individual woman, which denotes Neo-Indian womanhood in the United States of America. However, this same sex affair requires mention that Luce Irigary considers heterosexual intercourse, which usually prioritises the male force, a 'violation':

> an interruption of female autoerotic pleasure, as the penis forces apart the labia and forces female sexuality back into a phallic order, and "she calls this 'rape', naming heterosexual intercourse as foreign to feminine. (qtd.in Klages 108)

Gauri Mitra's lesbian attraction might have given a new identity had she not continued to intermittently recall her lives with Udayan Mitra and Subhas Mitra, both of whom can be considered as the representatives of the Indian patriarchy. By making this kind of same sex affair, Gauri had generated 'alternative version of herself', and her purpose was only 'to be alone in the end' (*The Lowland* 240). This same sex affair between Gauri and Lorna reminds the same sex affair between Celie and Shug as found in Alice walker's *The Color Purple* where she forges a sexual affinity with Celie by touching and kissing, and thus she gives Celie an accompaniment as she is bereft of such accompaniment due to her fascist husband. So, Shug is her mental support who fulfills the vacuum. Hence, loneliness or alienation actually creates a psychosomatic problem. Levinas believes while individual feels threatened by the weight of others freedom, s/he needs interaction and relationship with others to affirm his or her existence, which Gauri had a dire necessity; it indicates the possible reason of her alternative sexuality as well. Bela is fond of her father Subhas, and Gauri is thinking about the bad impact to be left upon her daughter after knowing the truth about her original father. In fact, the ghostly presence of Udayan is yet to be exterminated from her mind which gradually drifts her from everybody, especially from Subhas and Bela. Bela, being the second generation immigrants, is developing the idea of being courageous and self sufficient. Bela directly proclaims her mother, "You are as dead to me as he (Udayan) is." (*The Lowland* 320). It hurts Gauri's mind profusely and she feels alienated, she returns to Mumbai and watches Indian television programme, black-white films of sixties. Then she goes back to Kolkata in search of her roots where she seeks to meet Manas , her friend, and thus, she tries to renew her lost spirit within her old world, but she is alienated from her daughter, Bela and her husband, Subhas. However, Bela sends a letter in which it is stated:

> Meghna asks about you....you have taught me not to need you, and I don't need to know more about Udayan. But maybe, when Meghna is older, when she and I are both ready, we can try to meet again. (*ibid*.325)

Bela celebrates her alienation by researching on Hindu philosophy in which "the three tenses-past, present, future-were said to exist simultaneously in God. God was timeless, but time was personified as the god of death." (*ibid*.151). She continues with Descartes, who writes "that God recreated the body at each successive moment. So that time was a form of sustenance." (*ibid*.151). Bela's name is having affinity with Indian cultural heritage:

> Pronounced slightly differently, Bela's name, the name of a flower, was itself the world for a span of time, a portion of the day. Shakal bela meant morning; bikel bela, afternoon. Ratrirbela was night. (*ibid*.149)

Being a third generation immigrant, she still retains Indian cultural heritage by dint of her performances. Gauri is intimately alienated from Bela and her own cultural aspects, but she is living with the memories of her dead husband Udayan which are associated with the lowland. In fact, it is the lowland, where Udayan is killed, and the place acts as a metaphor in the novel which leads us to the Naxalite movement of 60s; thus it provides Gauri courage to sustain herself further: "Gauri sleeps with Subhas to extinguish Udayan's ghost. To smother what haunted her" (*ibid*.161). She sometimes even craves for Subhas's body,

> ...as she had craved odd combinations of food when she was pregnant. While she used to sit at home with her young daughter with Bela, she was aware of time not passing; of the sky nevertheless darkening at the end of another day. She was aware of the perfect silence in the apartment, replete with the isolation she and Bela shared. When she was with Bela, even if they were not interacting, it was as if they were one person, bound fast by a dependence that restricted her mentally, physically. At times it terrified her that she felt entwined and also so alone. (*ibid*.163)

In his book *The Dialogic Imagination* (1981), Mikhail Bakhtin invents the phrase 'chronotope' which contains a significant position in literary criticism. The term was first introduced as part of Albert Einstein's Theory of Relativity, and Bakhtin states that in literary criticism 'chronotope' indicates the "intrinsic connectedness of temporal and spatial relationships that are artistically expressed in literature" (84). Hence, space and time (as the fourth dimension of space) are inextricable, "fused into one carefully thought -out, concrete whole" (84). Chronotopes are instrumental in creating the narrative events of the novel. This literary trope, which has been deployed to provide a new critical angle to the novel, aims at materializing time in space. In fact,

> All the novel's abstract elements—philosophical and social generalizations, ideas, analyses of cause and effect–gravitate toward the chronotope and through it take flesh and blood, permitting the imaging power of art to do its work. Such is the representational significance of the chronotope. (Bakhtin 250)

What is significant in this chapter is the fact that several chronotopes often co-exist in a text or in several pieces of the same writer. Bakhtin explains: Within the limits of a single work and within the total literary output of a single author we may observe a number of different chronotopes and complex interactions among them, specific to the given work or author.

> Chronotopes are mutually inclusive, they co-exist, and they may be interwoven with, replace or oppose one another, contradict one another or find themselves in even more complex relationships. (252)

These interactions, which are always dialogical, often take place along the space-time continuum. This dialogue defines each narrative and "enters the world of the author, of the performer, and the world of the listeners and readers. And all of these worlds are chronotopic as well" (*ibid*.252). Therefore, the chronotopes of the world are basically performative, which are (re)created or (re)presented in the literary texts by the readers in various places, time zones, and so on. In Lahiri's first three published works, characters are prone to deal with the spatial aspects initially. They either want to return to the homeland, or obsessed with recreating a home in the United States of America. Some straddle geographical distances with more ease and negotiate transnational spaces adroitly. However, the basic thrust is surely on space. In *The Lowland*, however, there is a change from space to time, in the sense that Gauri settles without trouble in Rhode Island and then chooses to relocate to California, again without great efforts. Topographical distances or the buildings she lives in are less significant to her. Gauri is concerned with the past, especially. She is quite indifferent to the cartographical epistemology; she, in fact, inhabits through the memory of her dead husband, Udayan. For most of her life, she is preoccupied with the hermeneutics of time, and yearning to make hours flow backwards and have him by her side again. At the end of the novel, Gauri's path of life leads her back to Calcutta, where the temporal and spatial dimensions overlap, and she is able to coexist with the ghosts of the past. Lahiri has stated that with this novel she has arrived at the end of something she had been trying to work out in the course of her four published books. The story of the novel, which is set against the backdrop of 1960s India, exists at the beginning in Tollygunge, the poor neighbourhood where her father grew up, and dominated by a British country club. In so doing, she admits that she has not discussed such social and historical subjects earlier: "The Tollygunge Club was a metaphor for my own life and continues to be a metaphor for my life," Lahiri says in an interview with Andrew Keuler of *The Daily Free Press* (2014, para 4). "I have always felt like someone on the outside looking in", she continues, hinting at the issues of class, identity, and belonging (both in her childhood trips to India, and in her experience growing up in America). Individual and historical life sequences intermingle in this novel, more than in any other of her fictional works.

The writer goes back in time and space with a view to finishing a cycle and start her journey afresh. All her texts with their various spatial and temporal axes are intermeshed in a brilliant way: thus, it helps us look into Lahiri's oeuvre in its own chronotope. The metaphors she uses are indicative of immigration, and they are chronotopic in nature as well. In the last story from *Interpreter of Maladies*, immigration is compared to a journey into outer space, in *The Namesake,* it is delineated as a lifelong pregnancy, and in *Unaccustomed Earth* a character contemplates that immigration is identical to a life sentence of being foreign. Jhumpa Lahiri completed writing *The Lowland* in Rome, Italy, where she has visited with her family. "Italy is literally, geographically, in the middle, between India and the U.S.A. It is also culturally situated somewhere between these two societies", she acknowledges in an interview with Somak Ghoshal (2014, Para 28). Lahiri, in fact, inhabits in a third country or space, and thereby immersing herself in a third culture, which denotes different chronotopes. She claims that she does not seek her plots to be in a 'real' setting anymore. She does not even intend to retain the same issues or events (Indians abandoning their ancestral countries, the troubled historical and social realities that initiated their decision, the subsequent nostalgia that leaves scars on their lives, the hybridity of the second and third generations). She starts composing a fresh chapter in an attempt to write in Italy, yet her oeuvre can be placed in a new type of ethnic American writing. The future of ethnic fiction and identity, as it may be argued, subsides in the transnational sphere because it provides characters with an outlet from stifling social, historical, and psychological conditions. Indeed, all of Lahiri's narratives stress upon this liberating transnational pattern of belonging. In fine, the significant thing about Lahiri's fiction is the desire to contest the usual idea of absence and loss by which diaspora is characterised. For her identity is, in the words of Nigerian novelist Chris Abani, a destination. And such destination is dependent on the reiteration of performances on the part of immigrants, who are really in a way standing on the *postcolonial horizons*, having no cartographical epistemology.

In fact, the pathetic demise of Udayan has a poignant role to play throughout the whole novel. The ghost of Udayan not only haunts Gauri and other characters, rather tends to denote the years long history of the Naxalite Movement of 70s; it, consequently, indicates the pastiche of time and space and helps individuals re-view the intimate history in the recent time. Although Gauri seeks to adhere to the principles of foreign culture, she remains lost in the memory of Udayan. She seems to jostle with the real and the imaginary world, and thus blurs the distinction. Concomitantly, Udayan becomes everywhere. She appears to be epitomizing Bhabha's 'disjunctive temporality' which is synonymous with Rushdie's idea of 'broken mirror'. It results in the formation of 'fractured perception' of life which exemplifies her diasporic mental-setup. This novel brings out generational conflicts, history, memory, alternative sexuality, neo-Indian womanhood. In fact, the openendedness of the novel brings to the fore many possibilities of interpretation among the readers.

Chapter 5:

Celebration of *Italian Phase*: a new linguistic and cultural turn in *In Other Words*

Jhumpa Lahiri's sudden turn on to Italy is not only to suggest her intimacy with other language, but also for her multiple diasporic consciousness. Geographically, Italy is situated between India and the United States of America, which is smacking of *third space* to which she belongs freely and frankly. Being a diasporic writer, she always unsettles spacio-temporal barrier and from her last fiction *The Lowland* onwards, her fictional characters are also getting changed. Her sudden shift to *Italian phase* (emphasis added*)* and her attraction towards nonfiction is quite relevant to be reckoned with, which will help comprehend her fictional world. She does not want to cling to any particular culture and language. *In Other Words* (2016) is her memoir where she unveils her personal desire for re-world-ing her world through other words like Italian language directly. She desperately tries to ward herself off the influence of the English language. Linguistic ambivalence originates tension in her mind; her path to achieve knowledge regarding Italy and the language is quite tiresome and upheaval. But being a linguistic pilgrim how she attains it with the help of others has nicely been reflected here. Still, it seems her assimilation with the Italian language can be her strategic position which is put on or can be put off in the days to come to celebrate her ambivalent position as the work has been finished with lots of ambiguous questions.

Knowledge is almost like a limpid flow of a river and one needs to pass such river on his/her own. Such a journey is not so easy rather upheaval. It demands enormous concentration and self will to carry forward one's own dream to achieve the success. Lahiri is quite intent on learning Italian language out of her desire.

In Other Words, her first non-fictional-work-cum-memoir, is indicative of her revelation. Indeed, the process of learning Italian language seems to be vast like ocean. But out of her immense desire
to understand the language, she moves on being an alienated individual. However, to probe into the vast or unknown territory of
Italian language is adventurous and she is deriving pleasure out
of it. Other languages are always there to support her to comprehend Italian language. This is in fact an odyssey of a novice or an
intended learner to delve deep into the language and find out the
ins and outs of it, and thereby crossing the rebuffs to have attained
the ultimate knowledge regarding the Italian language. At the
very outset of the memoir, she is referring to the gradual devel-
opment of a novice learner, who has to cross the small river, has to
move on to reach another sea shore which is quite deep. She delineates her journey from an infant stage to her mature stage
where she ultimately gets the dream world. In fact, the entire
journey is replate with her self-will and being lonely, she is asking
for creating her fluid identity. She states, "I count the strokes, I
know that my companions are in the water with me, but I know
that each of us is alone" (*In Other Words* 4). In fact, the influence of
English language has always made an impact on her fondness for
Italian language; she seeks to negate her existence by maintaining
disinterestedness towards English and Bengali languages. Moreover, she is engaged rather in learning Italian languages through
her long association and patience with that language:

> For twenty years I studied Italian as if I were swimming along the edge of
> that lake. Always next to my dominant language, English. Always hugging
> that shore. It was good exercise. Beneficial for the muscles, for the brain,
> but not very exciting. If you study a foreign language that way, you won't
> drown. The other language is always there to support you, to save you. But
> you can't float without the possibility of drowning, of sinking. To know a
> new language, to immerse yourself, you have to leave the shore. Without a
> life vest. Without depending on solid ground. (*ibid.* 5)

Hence, Lahiri always rejects any unitary position being a diasporic
individual and linguistic pilgrim too, she moves on and on by
crossing manifold bars tied to the process of learning Italian lan-

guage; it signals her different journey with Italian language, which is termed by Mark Choate as 'italianita' (Choate 2).

Lahiri's engagement with the Italian language is basically out of her exorbitant desire for grasping the language, which tends her to fall into the dualism between her English language and her ongoing attempt to learn Italian language. Italian language seems to be reduced to being the object of desire and by identifying with this object, she becomes alienated from herself. She seeks to prune herself from the invariable influence of English language, and being a new comer in learning Italian language, she retains her tenacity by managing a dictionary. Wittgenstein believes that language is determining the nature of our experience. He feels that our behaviour and language merge in such a way that it invariably dictates our behaviour:

> What we call instructions, for example, or 'order', 'questions', 'answer', 'describing' etc is all bound up with very specific human actions and an order is only distinguishable as an order by means of the circumstances accompanying it. (qtd. in Wittgenstein 27)

So, Lahiri is yearning to know the Italian words to extend her knowledge further. Italian linguistic experience is consequently incumbent upon herself, which refers to a sort of dictation and limitation, too. In fact, she seems to say like Wittgenstein "The limits of my language mean the limits of my world" (qtd.in Wittgenstein 38). She proclaims,

> Every time I've been to Italy in the many years since, I've brought this dictionary with me. I always put it in my purse. I look up words when I'm in the street, when I return to the hotel after an outing, when I try to read an article in the newspaper. It guides me, protects me, explains everything. It becomes both map and a compass, and without it I know I'd be lost. It becomes a kind of authoritative parent, without whom I can't go out. I consider it a sacred text, full of secrets, of revelations. (*ibid.* 10)

Italy offers her more than solitude and it provokes her creative potential to come to the fore, and new Italian dictions increase her courage further:

> When you are in love, you want to live forever. You want the emotion, the excitement you feel to last. Reading in Italian arouses a similar feeling in

> me. I don't want to die, because my death would mean the end of my dis-
> covery of the language. Because every day, there will be a new word to
> learn. Thus true love can represent eternity. (*ibid*.45)

Her tremendous attraction towards dictionary to learn Italian language makes her more courageous, and continuously she goes on through the process of bracketing the influence of English language to hold her complete patience in learning Italian language:

> By now this small dictionary seems more like a brother than like a parent.
> And yet it's still useful to me, it still guides me. It remains full of secrets.
> This little book will always be bigger than I am. (*ibid*.12)

In the chapter "Love at First Sight", Lahiri is reminding of a trip to Italy in 1994 with her sister in which she brings out her unrequited love for Italian Language and Italy, too:

> I'm in an intimate, sober, joyful place. Shops decorated for the season. Nar-
> row, crowded streets, some more like corridors than like streets. There are
> tourists like my sister and me, but not many. I see the people who have
> lived here forever. They walk quickly, indifferent to the buildings. They
> cross the squares without stopping. (*ibid*.15)

In fact, she has given exquisite description of Italy where she refers to her love for her sister, and looks at the city with wonder. She states,

> ...my relationship with Italy is as auditory as it is visual. Although there
> aren't many cars, the city is humming. I'm aware of a sound that I like, of
> conversations, phrases, words that I hear wherever I go. As if the whole
> city were a theatre in which a slightly restless audience is chatting before
> the show begins. (*ibid*. 16)

In-fact, learning of the Italian language, according to Mark Choate, as the national language was a strategy to avert division in the expatriate communities. It stems from the different parts of Italy to regenerate in their minds the sentiments of Nationalism called Italian identity:

> Italian became pioneers in establishing a "global nation", beyond imperial
> control and territorial jurisdiction, held together by ties of culture, com-
> munications, ethnicity, and nationality. (Choate 2)

Lahiri seems to be obsessed with the Italian language, which tends to reformulate her identity as Italian. At the end of the story, she hardly considers her position to be stiff by resorting to the Italian language, but seeks to return to the United States of America. It, concomitantly, provides her ambivalent position.

People of Italy hardly pay any attention to the buildings, they cross the squares without stopping. Her interaction with Italy is visual only, but gradually, in spite of having difficulties in comprehending Italian words or language, she feels this language to be her own. In fact, a kind of inherent desire and attraction is writ large here. She feels a connection with this language:

> I feel fond. As if I had known it for years, even though there is still everything to discover. I would be unsatisfied, incomplete, if I didn't learn it. I realize that there is a space inside me to welcome it. I feel a connection and at the same time a distance. What I feel is something physical, inexplicable. It stirs an indiscreet, absurd longing. An exquisite tension. Love at first sight. (*ibid.*17)

Her passionate attitude towards Italy and the language propels her to move ahead and helps her ruminate her memories associated with the postcards, and the little gifts which she has brought with her from there to the United States of America. Indeed, her submission to the will of Italy and the language is her obsession and devotion, too, like the infatuation of a lover.

Lahiri with her diasporic sensibility is yet to be circumscribed to any specific time and location; she is drifting from one place to another. So, she does not belong to any particular linguistic category, be it Bengali, English or at present Italy: "Maybe because I'm a writer who doesn't belong completely to any language" (*ibid.*22). In fact, identity will always bear the trance of an exteriority that it cannot fully interiorize. 'I' am another means: 'I' cannot do without that other through whom 'I' get an 'I'. That 'other' becomes someone which 'I' cannot expel. In other words, my alienation is original, for it is implied in my self-constitution. There is no selfhood without foreign hood. The self is not something I possess, with an otherness that prevents me from being fully myself is infected with an otherness that prevents me from being fully at one with myself. Hence, Lahiri perceives such foreignness which has nicely been articulated while she states

> In my case there is another distance, another schism. I don't know Bengali perfectly. I don't know how to read it, or even write it. I have an accent. I speak without authority, and so I've always perceived a disjunction between it and me. As a result I consider my mother tongue paradoxically, a foreign language, too. (*ibid*.22)

Her purchasing of the book *Teach yourself Italian* itself testifies to her indomitable will power to learn the language on her own. She has tried her best to comprehend the language more clearly after exchanging Italian words with a salesman in Venice, but still she stumbles:

> I have to do all my interviews and presentations in English. There is always an interpreter next to me. I can more or less follow the Italian, but I can't express myself, explain myself, without English. I feel limited. What I learned in America, in the Classroom, isn't sufficient. My comprehension is so meagre that, here in Italy, it doesn't help me. The language still seems like a locked gate. I'm on the threshold, I can see inside, but the gate won't open. (24)

Macro and Claudia have been instrumental and helpful towards Lahiri to make her learned in that language, in spite of having her mistakes. In fact, looking at any object from the distance might place one in a state of separation. Lahiri's interaction with Italy occurs in a state of separation. She has cited examples of Dante, Ovid and their miserable individual journey amid alien sounds to arrive at her ultimate point. Her obsession towards the new language has helped her love the Italian culture, which consequently, bolsters her psyche.

Learning Italian language is a plea of the writer to understand such target language by disrupting source language or English language. Her journey of comprehending and learning is a tireless process. She thinks herself as a lone fighter who is seeking to cross the lake and is elated with joy in the true sense. To her, swimming is a good exercise like that of learning Italian language. Swimming being an exercise would strengthen one's own muscle:

Let's go back to the metaphor of the lake, the one I wanted to cross. Now I can walk into the water, up to my knees, up to my waist. But I still have to keep my feet on the bottom. That's just it, I'm forced to act like someone who doesn't know how to swim. (*ibid*.31)

She is persistent enough in carrying forward her interest towards the Italian language as she states:

My comprehension improves sporadically. The teacher is very encouraging, she says I speak the language well, she says I'll do fine in Italy. But it's not true. When I go to Milan, when I try to speak intelligently, fluently, I am always aware of the mistakes that hamper me, that confuse me, and I feel more discouraged than ever. (*ibid*.32)

She has read Alberto Moravia's *Gli Indifferenti* ('The Time of Indifference', 1929) and *La noia* ('Boredom', 1960), Cesare Pavese's *La Luna e i falo* ('The Moon and the Bonfires', 1949), the poetry of Salvatore Quasimodo (1901-68) and Umberto Saba (1883-1957), and always she wants to explore the unknown by challenging his own potential of understanding little bit of Italian language. Like Browning, she seems to unfurl "welcome each rebuff / That turns earth's smoothness rough," (*Rabbi Ben Ezra*, line no 31-32). In fact, difficulties in comprehending Italian language do not lead her towards inertia, but renders her *jouissance*: it is meted out in course of her patient perusal of those Italian texts. But, she cannot yet disown the influence of English language, which helps her revisit her divided personality:

In this period I feel like a divided person. My writing is nothing but a reaction, a response to reading. In other words, a kind of dialogue. The two things are closely bound, interdependent. Now, however, I write in one language and read exclusively in another. I am about to finish a novel, so I'm necessarily immersed in the text. It is impossible to abandon English. Yet my stronger language already seems behind me. (*In Other Words* 39)

It is said that hunger generates while hunger satiates. Lahiri is driven by her insatiable appetite for new Italian words, which sail her on and on to expand her knowledge on the Italian language. And such process of garnering new words is compared to the process of carrying a basket coupled with words. But, pouring woods into the basket signifies a productive value of it, but gathering words to extend her proficiency in that language is purely her passion: "I gather as many as possible. But it's never enough; I have an insatiable appetite" (ibid. 49). She further says, "My words seem more valuable than money. I am like a beggar who finds a pile of gold, a bag of jewels." (ibid. 50). She feels a strong affinity with words, but, she can hardly remember those words. But, still she believes in her deeds and her own efforts. Like Sisyphus, she believes in her potential and gathers words of various kinds being hardly anxious of forgetting many of them:

> All the words in the notebook are the sign of a physical, methodical growth. I think of my children's first weeks of life, when I went to the paediatrician every week to have their weight checked. Every ounce was recorded, evaluated. Each was concrete proof of their presence on the earth, of their existence. My understanding of Italian grows in a similar way. I acquire my vocabulary day by day, word by word. And yet my lexicon develops without logic, in a darting, fleeting manner. The words appear, accompany me for a while, then, often without warning, abandon me. (ibid. 52)

However, such abandonment seems to refer to Heidegger's concept of 'thrownness' (Heidegger XVIII) which develops human individual to lead one's life on her own by disdaining fate. Likewise, Lahiri's abandonment in terms of collecting new words seems to develop her potential more:

> The notebook contains all my enthusiasm for the language. All the effort. A space where I can wander, learn, forget, fail. Where I can hope" (ibid.52).

Utilisation of diary becomes another ploy, which she has mentioned to preserve Italian language, and it is a literary act of survival in the realm of Italian language:

> ...I were climbing a mountain. It's a sort of literary act of survival. I don't have many words to express myself-rather, the opposite. I'm aware of a state of deprivation. And yet, at the same time, I feel free, light. I rediscover the reason that I write the joy as well as the need. I find again the pleasure I've felt since I was a child: putting words in a notebook that no one will read. (ibid. 59)

In fact, diary has been quite instrumental in proving her good knowledge regarding the learning process of Italian language with discipline. But, diary writing makes her much more insular. The entire narration of her is interior or personal. She looks at the external world with her eye and delves deep into the objective world, and thus transgressing the world. Kant has divided human subjectivity into two halves, respectively, empirical ego and transcendental ego, which is conjoined through schema. Lahiri seeks to reworld the existing world by dint of her imaginative fiat. She is conforming to empirico-transcendental doublet. She herself says, "I think that a writer should observe the real world before imagining a non-existent one." (*ibid.* 63). In fact, her knowledge of English language has strongly embedded in her subconscious mind in such a way that she is unable to get rid of. But her persistence in knowing Italian language helps her move on and on like a soldier: "I rewrite everything like a lunatic until it satisfies me, while in Italian, like a soldier in the desert, I have to simply keep going" (*ibid.* 65). Lahiri being a translator is restless and yearning to have her ultimate goal. But, unknowingly, while she writes a story called 'The Exchange' in Italian language, she does not even know what she composes, but it really transcends its limitations.

Lahiri seeks to realise her own existence by celebrating her solitude. Indeed, such void yields her a vibrant stimulation to confront anxieties of the present society:

> She wanted to live in solitude, like a monk, in order to confront what she couldn't bear. To her friends, her family, the man who loved her, she said that she had to go away for a while (*ibid.* 70).

In fact, solitude does not bring negative vibes in her mind, rather yields motion to her life. Considering herself to be imperfect and deriving positive stimuli from such imperfections provide mobility to her identity. It refers to a journey of Lahiri from Being to Becoming. In fact, she is in Dionysian state which propels her to move on towards Apollonian stage, continuously. Her indomitable desire to go for Italian language can be a matter of criticism to many, but she averts such herd mentality by yielding an extra push to her wish and will. Solitude becomes more desirable to her than anything, which demands creative indulgence on her part to produce something new:

> She walked for hours, wandered aimlessly, without speaking...When she
> was hungry, she ate something sitting on a bench. When she was tired, she
> went to the movies. She imagined she was a falling leaf, like every oth-
> er...She was suspended in time, like a person without a shadow. And yet
> she was alive, she felt more alive than eve. (*ibid.* 71)

As the imperfection leads one to be perfect, similarly inconsistent
life leads one to realise one's own potential to be consistent, which
Lahiri seems to articulate here. Extricating oneself from the onrush
linguistic inconveniences are not pertinent to her, rather she is
absorbed in comprehending that language with pure patience and
concentration. Translation means an alteration of human individual in order to give a new light to the other language. Translation
is related to her prominent entity to negate source language, and
yearning for knowing the target language. Being a linguistic nomad, she is continuously translating herself to keep up her foreignness: "She was a foreigner, like the translator" (*ibid.* 73). Being
a novice learner of Italian language, she seeks to create her existence on her own, desperately, with a hope to be an appropriate
learner. It starts with lots of imperfections. Translator is always
referring to the another version of oneself, and a translator always
tries to curtail his/her self from any spacio-temporal, cultural
hegemony which Lahiri does: "The translator felt disconcerted,
empty. She had come to that city looking for another version of
herself, a transfiguration." (*ibid.*77). Lahiri has mentioned: "And
whether I write as an American or an Indian, about things American or Indian or otherwise, one thing remains constant: I translate
therefore I am" ("Intimate Alienation" 5) which denotes her to be
a cultural translator, and similarly she is a linguistic translator,
too. By means of translating herself, she seems to be a linguistic
nomad, and it becomes her survival strategy also: "Almost all of
my characters are translators, insofar as they must make sense of
the foreign to survive" (*ibid.*5). Harish Trivedi rightly points out
"this echoes, probably unwittingly, the Benjaminian-Derridean
sur-vivre (6). Hence, Lahiri herself asserts that "translation is not
only a finite linguistic act but an ongoing cultural one" (*ibid.*5). She
herself proclaims,

> When I read in Italian, I feel like a guest, a traveller. Nevertheless, what I'm doing seems a legitimate, acceptable task. When I write in Italian, I feel like an intruder, an imposter. The work seems counterfeit, unnatural. I realize that I've crossed over a boundary, that I feel lost, in flight. I'm a complete foreigner. When I give up English, I give up my authority. I'm shaky rather than secure. I'm weak. What is the source of the impulse to distance myself from my dominant language, the language that I depend on, that I come from as a writer, to devote myself to Italian?. (*In Other Words* 81)

Lahiri feels quite tensed and feeble by starting her life in Italian Language anew. It relegates the position of her English language, so she says, "How is it possible that when I write in Italian I feel both freer and confined, constricted?"(*ibid.* 83).But, still she has enormous courage to write in Italian language, in spite of having lots of imperfections because she believes "the need to write always comes from desperation, along with hope" (*ibid.* 83).In fact, desperation emanates from the void, and the desire drives her to make herself attached with the Italian language. She is in search of creating her existence in the realm of Italian language. She clarifies her desire and impulse of writing in Italian language by stating:

> Why do I write? To investigate the mysteries of existence. To tolerate myself. To get closer to everything that is outside of me...Writing is my only way of absorbing and organizing life. (*ibid.* 84)

At the end she gets to realise that,

> ...as a word can have many dimensions, many nuances, great complexity, so, too, can a person, a life. Language is the mirror, the principal metaphor. Because ultimately the meaning of a word, like that of a person, is boundless, ineffable. (*ibid.* 84)

Learning Italian language perfectly becomes a mirage to her. The impossibility of learning of that language does not bring unhappiness, rather renders her immense courage to move on to reach out to the apex of it by means of her writing:

> I have to accept the impossibility of reaching the height that inspires me but at the same time pushes me into a corner. Now the height is not the work of a writer more brilliant than I am but, rather, the heart of the language itself. Impossibility and wandering lead one to be more creative: "I have to accept the impossibility of reaching the height that inspires me but at the same time pushes me into a corner. Now the height is not the work

of a writer more brilliant than I am but, rather, the heart of the language it-self. Although I know that I will never be securely inside that heart, I try, through writing, to reach it. (*ibid.* 88)

Familiar words are referring to limitation where she falls into. Keeping oneself from distance augments creativity. However such un-attainability leads one to be alienated to generate something: "Without a sense of marvel at things, without wonder, one can't create anything" (*ibid.* 90).

In fact, impossibility is more desirable to her to attain courage which makes her a linguistic nomad: "If everything were possible, what would be the meaning, the point of life? If it were possible to bridge the distance between me and Italian, I would stop writing in that language" (*ibid.* 91). She also feels "...writing is an extended homage to imperfection" (*ibid.* 108). Imperfection is, she thinks of, the source of inspiration, invention, imagination, stimulation and creativity. She believes "The more I feel imperfect, the more I feel alive" (*ibid.* 109). She considers herself more as a divided subject due to her split personality: "Because of my divided identity, or perhaps by disposition, I consider myself an incomplete person, in some way deficient" (*ibid.* 107).

In fact, her interaction with the Italian language seems to be referring to Lacanian concept of *Suturing* (405) which demands continuous performances on her part with the Italian language, resulting in her mobile subjectivity. Suture essentially becomes subjectivised through a structure between the subject of the signifier and the signifying structure. This is indeed a mending process where self-other dialectic is at work, leading towards infinity. Lahiri's interaction with the Italian language on a daily basis is almost like a trial and error process through which she constructs and crosses the bridge:

> Every sentence I write in Italian is a small bridge that has to be constructed, then crossed. I do it with hesitation mixed with a persistent, inexplicable impulse. Every sentence, like every bridge, carries me from one place to another. It's an atypical, enticing path. a new rhythm. Now I'm almost used to it. (*In Other Words* 98)

The never ending fissure between the Italian and English language makes her perplexed:

> Compared with Italian, English seems overbearing, domineering, full of itself. I have the impression that English has been in captivity and, having just been released, is furious. Probably, feeling neglected for almost a year, it's angry at me. The two languages confront each other on the desk, but the winner is already more than obvious. The translation is devouring, dismantling the original text. I'm struck by how this bloody struggle exemplifies the theme of the festival, the very subject of the piece. (*ibid.* 113)

Lahiri is now absorbed in the Italian language vehemently, and frantically tries to protect it under her cover like a new-born baby. English, which appears to be *hairy adolescent* to her, peeps into the Italian periphery to disturb its little brother like Italian language. In fact, she defines her dual identity comparing herself as a mother:

> Now as I translate myself, I feel like the mother of two children. I notice that I've changed my relation to the language, but maybe this change reflects a development, natural journey. One type of love follows the other; from a passionate coupling, ideally, a new generation is born. I feel an emotion even more intense, more pure, more transcendent for my children. Maternity is a visceral bond, an unconditional love, a devotion that goes beyond attraction and compatibility. (*ibid.*114)

She feels that translation is not only translating any text into another language, but it suggests transcreation, too, which is nothing but a rebirth of a new child. By translating, she can intimately associate herself with that language, alienating herself from the source language, which yields to her a separate space, a separate identity:

> I think that translating is the most profound, most intimate way of reading. A translation is a wonderful, dynamic encounter between two languages, two texts, two writers. It entails a doubling, a renewal. I used to love translating from Latin, from ancient Greek, from Bengali. It was a way of getting close to different languages, of feeling connected to writers very distant from me in space and time. (*ibid.*115)

While Lahiri goes back to the United States of America leaving Rome, Italy appears in her mind as a home. She has really been suffering from homesickness:

> After spending a year in Rome I return to America for a month. Immedi-
> ately, I miss Italian. Not to be able to speak it and hear it every day distress
> me. When I go to restaurants, to shops, to the beach, I'm irritated: Why
> aren't people speaking Italian? I don't want to interact with anyone. I have
> an aching sense of homesickness. (*ibid.* 119)

She feels doubly alienated while she is in Italy as she feels the lack
of English, and now while she comes to Italy, she feels the lack of
the Italian influence. Such melancholia emanates from the loss,
leading her towards mourning:

> Now I feel a double crisis. On the one hand I'm aware of the ocean, in eve-
> ry sense, between me and Italian. On the other, of the separation between
> me and English. I'd already noticed it in Italy, translating myself. But I
> think that emotional distance is always more pronounced, more piercing,
> when, in spite of proximity, there remains an abyss. (*ibid.*122)

In fact, the true intellectuals, according to Edward Said, must be
performing the role of an *amateur* (207). In fact, an amateur is
somebody who will live fully, yet with a disinterested engagement with ideas and values. Lahiri seems to be sounding the
same. Her exilic condition is metaphoric, which is not disconnected from a homeland, but demonstrates a willing homesickness
through specific strategies and techniques:

> Without a homeland and without a true mother tongue, I wander the
> world, even at my desk. In the end I realize that it wasn't a true exile: far
> from it. I am exiled even from the definition of exile. (*In Other Words* 124)

Lahiri laments over the physical appearance which seems to be
deterrent in explicating herself as an apt Italian speaker: "Don't
touch our language, some Italians seem to say to me. It doesn't
belong to you" (*ibid.* 131). Linguistic and cultural hegemony of
Italy germinates a border where she is caught into. Her husband is
applauded for being fluent in speaking Italy, but in spite of having
her capability of speaking in Italy, she is considered as *other* in the
eyes of mainstream country:

> How is it that you speak Italian so well? And I have to provide an explana-
> tion, I have to say why. The fact that I speak Italian seems to them unusual.
> No one asks my husband that question. (*ibid.*131)

Such linguistic and cultural b/order seeks to circumscribe her identity. And being a linguistic and cultural nomad, she usually faces the same problem in America. In India too, she is continuously asked "Where are you from". She expresses her fume being not recognised her to be Italian: "They don't understand me because they don't want to understand me; they don't understand me because they don't want to listen to me, accept me. That's how the wall works" (*ibid.* 130). In her interview with Sheila Pierce, she asserts that "I wanted a very long time to really go away from the world I knew...Rome has given me a sense of belonging...Here, I'm able to accept myself in way that I haven't ever been to in the United States or India because these two sides were always at war. Having been born in London to Bengali parents, and raised in Rhode Island from the age of two, Lahiri says she felt eternally torn between the language in which she was educated (English) and the language in which she was raised (Bengali). I have uprooted myself not only from a physical place but also from a linguistic place. This double uprooting is artistic freedom, and it's dizzying. Once you taste that you can't give it up." So, naturally being a creative writer, she always tries to topple the linguistic wall:

> I write in order to break down the wall, to express myself in a pure way. When I write, my appearance, my name has nothing to do with it. I am heard without being seen, without prejudices, without a filter. I am invisible. I become my words, and the words become me. (*ibid.*133)

Such inquisitiveness is quite pertinent in exploring her disinterestedness towards any particular culture and language. Her continuous battle with the Italian language inspires her to tinker her existence again and again: "...linguistic wall, however exasperating, interests me, inspires me" (*ibid.* 134). As Sheila Pierce states that Lahiri in an interview says "What I was wanting to get away from in moving to Rome was the sense of me being an expert...Here, I have felt free and invisible, and have felt the sense that there there's another mountain to climb, I' am at the bottom of it, and that's the great challenge."

Lahiri becomes experimental in terms of exhibiting herself in the realm of language. Her growing up with the Bengali language, her adherence to English language, and of late her immersion into the Italian language prepare the ground of linguistic triangle- all these refer to the hegemony of each language. But her choice of Italian language is her pure passion:

> The arrival of Italian, the third point on my linguistic journey, creates a tri-
> angle. It creates a shape rather than a straight line. A triangle is a complex
> structure, a dynamic figure. The third point changes the dynamic of that
> quarrelsome old couple. I am the child of those unhappy points, but the
> third does not come from them. It comes from my desire, my labour. It
> comes from me. I think that studying Italian is a flight from the long clash
> in my life between English and Bengali. A rejection of both the mother and
> the step mother. An independent path. (*ibid*. 141)

Though her engagement with the language is emanating from her absolute desire, but still she feels the coexistence of both the Bengali and English in her mind: "Although I'm fleeing, I realize that both English and Bengali are beside me. Just as in triangle, one point leads inevitably to another" (*ibid*.142). Hence, Harish Trivedi rightly asserts, "in this postcolonial-postmodernist world, where newness constantly enters through cultural translation" (7). And the perceived newness like hybridised linguistic and cultural state to which Lahiri belongs is identifiably referring to what Benjamin called "Untranslatability" (Trivedi 5). However, her continuous identification with the mirror to construct her ego is fleeting her personality and leading her towards void or emptiness, which seems to be her inspiration. She negates her existence strategically to dismantle any kind of cultural and linguistic border. Her abso-lute freedom and will power helps her to be alienated from any socio-politico-cultural and linguistic hegemony, and thereby pro-voking her creative impulse to come to the fore:

> I come from that void, from that uncertainty. I think that the void is my
> origin and also my destiny. From that void, from all that uncertainty,
> comes the creative impulse. The impulse to fill the frame. (*ibid*.144)

In order to substantiate her insatiable desire for the Italian lan-guage, and her indebtedness to English and Bengali language, she is referring to her gradual transformation being a writer. She is very much fond of Ovid's *Metamorphoses* (c. A.D. 8). Hence, she brings the analogy of Daphne and Apollo and shows how Daphne becomes a laurel tree with a view to protect herself from the hands of Apollo, now Daphne is free to lead her life being a tree. Apollo can touch her, but cannot possess her. Metamorphosis becomes her salvation. Likewise, she tries her luck to interpret herself in a new language to reinvent her identity. She feels "Metamorphosis is a process that is both violent and regenerative, a death and a birth. It's not clear where the nymph ends and the tree begins; the beauty of this scene is that it portrays the fusion of two elements, of both beings" (149). She repeatedly seeks to repudiate the influence of the English language which impedes her journey: "English denotes a heavy, burdensome aspect of my past. I'm tired of it" (*ibid*. 151). She holds her faith and interest severely in learning Italian language by disdaining immense reputation and recognition garnered through English language:

> I became a famous writer. I received a prize that I was sure I did not deserve, that seemed to me a mistake. Although it was an honour, I remained suspicious of it. I couldn't connect myself to that recognition, and yet it changed my life. (*ibid*, 145)

She feels "...Italian, covers me like a kind of bark. I remain inside: renewed, trapped, relieved, uncomfortable". (*ibid*.150).

She continuously tries to destroy herself to reconstruct herself in a new language:

> As a writer I can demolish myself. I can join words together and work on sentences without ever being considered an expert. I'm bound to fail when I write in Italian, but, unlike my sense of failure in the past, this doesn't torment or grieve me. (*ibid*.151)

In fact, conforming to the theory of *impersonality* (Lee 1), the writer tries to enter into the objective world in order to surpass the objective reality and make it transcendental one by means of her imaginative fiat. Her continuous metamorphosis being a linguistic pilgrim is stemming from her absolute invisibility: "All my writing comes from a place where I feel invisible, inaccessible" (*ibid*. 154).

But, she also realises, "A total metamorphosis isn't possible in my case. I can write in Italian, but I can't become an Italian writer...It's not possible to become another writer, but it might be possible to become two" (*ibid*. 154).

Lahiri's ceaseless effort to investigate her aptitude in the Italian language is an ongoing process, having no specific destination. Now she has matured herself up while her Italian language is formulated by "an amalgam of writers, of various historical epochs, who write in diverse styles" (*ibid*. 162). But, still she feels that the usual flavour of Italian language is somehow missing. She is very much concerned and dissatisfied, too, due to her ups and downs of the Italian vocabulary:

> Like the tide, my vocabulary rises and falls, comes and goes. The words added every day in the notebook are transient. I spend an hour choosing the right one, but then, often, I forget it. Now when I encounter an unfamiliar word in Italian I already know several terms, also in Italian, to express the same thing. (*ibid*. 163)

She again says, "I do my best to hit the target, but when I take aim I never know where the arrow will land" (*ibid*. 163). She has gone through tremendous upheaval to constitute her identity to be an Italian writer: "I have to withstand those stormy moments when the sky darkens, when I despair, when I fear I'm at the end of my rope." (*ibid*. 164). However, her investigation is a continuous process which is premised upon basically her performances. Her attachment with the language and detachment, too, falls her into a buffer zone. Such detachment probably leads her towards uncertainty, and tends her to be a benevolent and meticulous researcher. This is what is referring to her ultimate immersion into it, which is utopian indeed, and there is always the point of reverting back. She herself proclaims,

> Investigating my discovery of the language, I think I have investigated myself. The verb 'sondare' means 'to explore, to examine'. It means, literally, to measure the depth of something. According to my dictionary the verb means 'seek to know, to understand something, in particular the thoughts and intentions of others. It implies detachment, uncertainty; it implies a state of immersion. It means methodical, stubborn research, into something that remains forever out of reach. (*ibid*. 165)

In fact, her struggle to make her existence in terms of Italian language is an ongoing process; the support whatever she has got from them is really laudable, and is compared to 'scaffolding'.

Indeed, solitude, according to my interpretation, seems to be the ultimate desire of Lahiri. This helps her to be intimate with her own world. Linguistic ambivalence perceptively puts her in a buffer zone; a tension is always engulfed with her psyche about what to do at the time of her arrival in the United States of America again. Her close association with Italy for three years evokes a strong attachment with the language, which yields her enough scope to explore herself explicitly. Whenever she is asked if her earlier fictional-writings were autobiographical or fictional in the true sense of the term, she feels awkward. She unfurls her rage as she always lingers for creative space by delimiting her position. Her creation of *The Lowland* is her continuous research of the realistic event like Naxalite movement and the place Kolkata, too, in which she was not present during her writing. However, such distance always tends her to bring out creativity. By infusing reality and imagination, she always seems to make her world transnational, borderless and hybrid, too. She herself says,

> Invention can also be a trap. A character fabricated out of nothing has to seem like a real person-there's the challenge. It was a challenge, especially in *The Lowland*, to portray a real place where I have never lived, and to evoke a historical era that I didn't know. I did a lot of research to make that world, that time, believable. Beginning with my first book I evoked Calcutta, my parents' native city. Because it was, for them, a far-off place that had almost disappeared, I was looking for a way, through writing, to bridge the distance, and to make it present. (*ibid.*197)

But usage of the Italian language broaches much more freedom for her in this context:

> Writing in Italian, I feel that my feet are no longer on the ground...In this book language is not only the tool but the subject. Italian remains the mask, the filter, the outlet, the means. The detachment without which I can't create anything. And it's this new detachment that helps me show my face. (*ibid.* 198)

Hence, her *Italian phase* [my own emphasis] seems to refer to her shift from her fictional to the non-fictional world, and she is obsessed with her own Italian world where she thinks of herself absolutely free; although she is not sure whether she will stick to her *Italian phase* or return to her former place, the United States of America. In fact, a tension of loss and gaining is embedded in her subconscious mind, which is also articulated in her memoir:

> Should I continue on this road? Will I abandon English definitively for Italian? Or, once I'm back in America, will I return to English? How would I return to it? I know from my parents that, once you've left, you're gone forever. If I stop writing in Italian, if I go back to working in English, I expect to feel another type of loss. (*ibid.* 203)

She is utterly confused about whether she should stay in Italy and cling on to the Italian culture or she should go back to the United States of America. Her perennial ambiguity comes to the fore while she is caught in the linguistic as well as cultural dilemma. But her adherence to the *Italian phase* and non-fiction writing mark a change in her works. It opens up a new vista in the Lahirivian oeuvre.

CONCLUSION

Jhumpa Lahiri exalts her objectivity in looking at the World; since her world is divided into many, she cannot stick to any particular Nation, language and culture. She believes in translating herself as well as her fictional characters to anticipate transnationalism and transnation, too. In fact, such propensity of transnationalism in the case of Lahiri is akin to her self-alienation from any specific carto-graphical epistemology. However, "Translation is neither the life nor the death of the text, only or already its living on, its life after-life" (Derrida 83). Translation is a very vital trope to lead towards Trans (Nation) and transnationalism. In fact, the prefix 'trans' has been rediscovered in the realm of 'transnationalism' where "dias-pora is described as involving the production and reproduction of transnational social and cultural phenomena." (Vertovec 153). Migrants by means of their ceaseless effort of translation become 'transmigrants' (Mishra 174) who are not belonging to any par-ticular place, rather assuming the strata called global citizens. However, the coexistence of various cultures within a specific place is conforming to the concept of multiculturalism. But, it should not be 'plural monoculturalism' (Sen 156), which refers to the formation of the distinct group boundaries, and Amartya Sen has vituperated such sectarian attitude in his *Identity and Violence* (2003). It rather refers to cosmopolitan citizenship and "such a perspective sees a value in maintaining ethnic diversity, but at the same time contends that individuals ought to be in a position to pick and choose from multiple cultures" (Kivisto 37). Like other Diasporic novelists, Jhumpa Lahiri also explicates her notion that she does not want to fix herself within a particular place, culture and language, and thus indicates her nomadic nature. Homi Bha-bha in his essay "DissemiNation: Time, narrative, and the margins of the modern nation" has brought in the concept of untranslata-bility by referring to Walter Benjamin's *The Task of the Translator:*

> Fragments of a vessel in order to be articulated together must follow one another in the smallest details although they need not to be like one anoth-er. In the same way a translation, instead of making itself similar to the

meaning of the original, it must lovingly and in detail, form itself according to the manner of meaning of the original, to make them both recog-
nizable as fragments of the greater language, just as fragments are the broken parts of the vessel. (320)

However, the act of cultural translation is very much akin to the
condition of human migration. In fact, cultural dissociation is related to the untranslatability. Being a cultural translator, Jhumpa
Lahiri in her essay "Intimate Alienation: Immigrant Fiction and
Translation" (2002) puts penchant importance on diasporic subjectivity which does not epitomise any kind of fixity. The effusion of
her very essay is translation, which is an important tool used by
herself as well as her fictional characters to prove her and her fictional characters' stature as 'foreign', 'non existent' or 'nomadic'
so far as survival mechanism is concerned. She also states that
almost all her characters are translators, "insofar as they must
make sense of the foreign in order to survive" (Lahiri, "Intimate"
5). Lahiri's survival mechanism relies in her literary transgression.
Her love for preparing a contingent zone for her own self brings
out her ontology of liminality which finds its resonance in her
own literary motto, "I translate therefore I am" (Lahiri, "Intimate
Alienation" 5) which is attuned to the Cartesian proposition "I
think therefore I am". However, apropos of the Lahiri fiction, it is
crystal clear that her take on translation is a process related to the
heterogeneity of diasporic subjectivity. While subjectivity is concerned, it needs to be started from Kantian notion of subjectivity
which is ramified into two halves—empirical ego and transcendental subjectivity. But standing on postmodern condition, Lyotard has placed subjectivity at institutional 'nodal points' which is
constructed within a mobile 'fabric of relations and practices'
(Lyotard15), referring to the pluralistic notion of Subjectivity; it
defies Kantian binarization of subjectivity prevalent up to Eight-
eenth century. On the cultural parlance, Simon Gikandi also
thinks of liminality in terms of diasporic subjectivity formation
which is defined as 'global flow' (675). Such global flow is being
resonated in the global soul, Jhumpa Lahiri whose negotiation
with the Euro American Culture as well as with the ethnic culture
unsettles space-time continuum, geopolitical and cultural barrier.

Hence, thinking of herself as being and translating herself as an individual broaches polyphonic voices and evolves a sense from Being to Becoming. To Lahiri, diasporic subjectivity is a kind of journey steeped in loss, gain and destination. In fact, the spatial and cultural dislocation which can be felt in her debut short story collection 'Interpreter of Maladies: Stories of Bengal, Boston and Beyond' where the title itself suggests a transnationalism or beyondness. It becomes overt while it is premised upon transcultural encounter, referring to the cultural, linguistic and psychological alienation, too. Mrs Sen is portrayed as an alienated individual, who forges neo-nativism being completely dislocated from the host culture by means of performing her ancestral cultural tools. Shoba and Shukumar are being haunted by the loss of their offspring; it tends them to create a temporary intimate space, which really offers a confrontation between utopia and reality. Dev's beautiful description of her wife who resembles the beauty of Madhuri Dixit, the Indian film actress, generates a sexual jealousy in Miranda, and thereby invariably challenges Saidean stereotypical relationship between occident and orient. It seems to be felt more while by referring to Bell Hook's concept of 'Eating the other', it is being shown here that being a woman of white culture how she is lured by the orient like Dev and orient culture, too. It indicates probably neo-orientalism where primitive becomes 'exotic' which engulfs the lady. The relationship between Lilia and Pirzada completely depends on imaginary level in spite of having the hurly burly of partition. It actually exhibits how emotion vindicates ingeniously a close rapport between individual and social space. It further showcases how individual has to surrender to the will of social taboos. So, Lilia cannot be truly separated from Pirzada because she continuously goes on to relive via her imaginary world, which signifies the 'third space'. Mr Kapasi being the interpreter always assumes an in-between space to articulate the multilingual feelings of different people. His interpretation of the maladies of Mrs Das seems to generate a very close world between them as they have been suffering from the loss. But still, being an interpreter, he feels empathetic towards her, which has been interpreted by referring to the concept of Scarry's Body in *pain*. Bibi Halder, the victim of Indian societal rituals, gets subjugated in such patriarchal norms. After the demise of her husband, she gets married to somebody; it segregates her from the orthodox culture. This situation can be compared to the *sado-rituals* by Mary Daly. But by bringing in Nietzschean concept of *will to power*, she has been represented as an utterly enthusiastic lady, who moves on to create her entity. On the other hand, Boori Maa has been transmuted into the *docile body* and oppressed as subaltern, being forcibly migrated from her country. However, she has always been haunted as if by the Hobbesian ghost of nation-state ideology and conforms to the situation of 'bare life' or *state of exception*. Such alienation makes her retrogressive towards her home through memory. And "The Third and Final Continent" itself testifies to the spatial overlapping of the fictional characters leading towards the *third space*. However, such nine stories explicate the sense of loss, marital discord, communication under the soft veneer of migrant experience. The subtitle 'Stories of Bengal, Boston and Beyond' refers to the transnational traits of her characters, who are straddling between two or more linguistic worlds. Lahiri herself proclaims in her essay "Intimate Alienation: Immigrant Fiction and Translation" that "I am the first one to admit my knowledge of India is limited, the way in which all translations are..." (5). Her act of translation and representation of India is nothing but sharing her self-representation. Through translation one can gain something and can lose something:

> It is normally supposed that something always gets lost in translation; I cling, obstinately, to the notion that something always gets lost in translation; I cling, obstinately, to the notion that something can also be gained. (Rushdie 17)

Unaccustomed Earth, her second short story collections, consists of eight stories, unearthing the transplanted identity and deviation from Hawthorne's concept of having a complete domination of father over children. Rather it seeks to track down the generational gap between the first and second generation immigrants, mostly and cross cultural milieu her characters are caught in. Ruma is an emigrant, who has shifted from India to the U.S.A. and wants to adopt to the American culture. But her father's abrupt arrival in her place seems to be threatening to her private space, coupled with oedipal tension. Her father's appearance tends her to relive her mother-figure and motherland, too. However, such dialectic between self and M(other) is leading Lahiri's characters towards infinity. Such shadow of mother seems to engulf Kaushik's mind, too, which seems to generate the concept of 'secret buried alive' (qtd. in Munos 33) regarding his deceased mother-figure in his mind, resulting in his alienation. On the other hand, the cultural clash becomes quite potent where westernised Hema, an individual lady, becomes completely dislocated, and the death of her childhood friend Kaushik whom she used to love, makes her repentant, and thereby tending her to create her space imbued with the memory of her remembered past. The story more or less refers to the cultural pastiche of memory and space. Postcards from various countries are bearing the significance of blurring any specific place and culture also. 'Hell and Heaven' seeks to locate a cultural dislocation and place her fictional characters in the foreign territory where Pranab and Aparna have made a unity in terms of their cultural solidarity. But Pranab's sudden shift to Deborah, an American lady, creates a disruption between them, though he breaks down his relationship with Deborah too- all these encapsulate a patriarchal domination, women subjugation and his absolute ambivalent position also. The entire short story collection deals with the cultural dislocation, transgenerational phantoms, postmemory which are reverberating, in a way, intimate alienation.

In *The Location of Culture* (1994), Bhabha writes that to be 'unhomed' does not mean to be homeless, yet it is difficult to accommodate the 'unhomely' in the familiar division between the private and public spheres. In the process of displacement ,"the borders between home and world become confused; and, uncannily, the private and public become part of each other, forcing upon us a vision that is as divided as it is disorienting" (9). Lahiri's fictional character like Ashima refers to such beyondness because Ashima means, in Bengali, borderless; Boundary is a "place from which something begins its presencing in a movement not dis-

similar to the ambulant, ambivalent articulation of the beyond"
(Bhabha 5). However, Ashima is oscillating between the India and
America after the demise of her husband which yields her a transnational nuance. In fact, home is bereft of the cartographical epistemology, which is generated by dint of imaginative fiat, and
thereby making the very concept of home "the mythic place of
desire" (Brah 192). I have sought to exhibit here how the name of
the novel can be *Nameshake* instead of *The Namesake*, as Gogol is
continuously combating between the Indian and American culture
and his close association with the Russian name Nikhil (who en-
compasses all) has made him confused or ABCD (American Born
Confused Desi). The concept of naming is also involved with the
colonial ideology and how such naming can be analysed by bringing in the Spivakian concept of *catachresis*, has been discussed
here. By bringing in Anita Mannur's concept of *Culinary citizenship*, it has been shown how food becomes a vital metaphor referring to the cultural hybridity. While Ashima is preparing 'Jhalmuri' during her pregnancy, it smacks of her reincarnation of Indigenous culture in the alien shore, on the other hand, she is also
preparing Sandwich with the roast beef for her children Gogol
and Sonai (Second Generation Immigrants), indicating hybridised
culture. In fact, Gogol, Sonai, Moushumi are the harbinger of cosmopolitanism. Family has taken a very important space in the
immigrant location where cultural rituals and religious rites are
performed by the community to maintain one's own ethno cultural values which are inimical to the host culture. In fact, the ultimate destination of the second generation immigrants is aporetic
and the constitution of their individual self is being generated
through 'dialectic' and 'difference'. In fact, the continuous deferral
of Diasporic individuals disrupt the hegemonic binary between
the home and the host, the local and the global, and thereby making her characters fluid.

Jhumpa Lahiri in her *The Lowland* is rife in explicating her fictional characters under the soft veneer of Naxalite Movement in
which diasporic loss, gain and destination are represented to topple discursive mapping. They are, to put in the words of Bill Ashcroft, conforming to the concept of the *postcolonial horizons*, which

connotes alterity and possibilities. In fact, I have tried to reveal here as to how the death of Udayan becomes a *spirit*, which appears repeatedly throughout the entire story, and thereby leading us to feel how Naxalite history and individuality are coalesced together to render us the Lahirian chronotopes. Moreover, there is a subtle alteration perceived in the field of gender orientation in *The Lowland*. In her "Sexy", *The Namesake*, "A Temporary Matter", "The Treatment of Bibi Halder", "Unaccustomed Earth", Lahiri is out and out explicit in making her fictional characters self-sufficient to choose their partners which is certainly referring to the gross heteronormativity. But in her *The Lowland*, she, for the first time, deviates from her heteronormative love affair and yields a new vista in terms of gender orientation; Gauri's sexual intimacy with Lorna seems to be sounding the same-sex affair and quest for alternative space also. In fact, this is probably another kind of translation she has tried to make here through her fictional characters, which of course tends her to generate as well as celebrate her alienation also.

However, certain changes can be felt in terms of her writing from *The Lowland* onwards. In fact, she has finished her novel in Rome, Italy where she has shifted with her family. In her interview with Somak Ghosal she admits "Italy is literally, geographically, in the middle, between India and the U.S.A. It is culturally situated somewhere between these two societies" (2014, paragraph 28). However, her attempt to write in Italy and her enormous love for Italy is adumbrating her new journey which I have termed *Italian phase* (Emphasis added). Delving deep into a new language having no knowledge, she strives for reading, writing and comprehending the language which indicate her nomadic existence or transnational pattern of her belonging which is very much tied to her essay 'Intimate Alienation: Immigrant Fiction and Translation". She develops an intimacy with the Italian language and her journey is arduous enough with lots of imperfections. And she also suffers from the anxiety of influence stemming from her first language like English that appears as a deterrent for learning Italian language. Thus, by dint of her own will, she seeks to create her own world by making herself intimately alienated from the first language, thus yielding her a new strata called *other word*. At the end of her memoir *In Other Words,* she still becomes confused whether she should stay in Italy or go to America. In fact, such linguistic tension or ambivalent subjectivity is still overt here. Her gradual shift from fiction to non-fiction does not refer to her fixed position; she might alter her position in times to come. However, in her recent non-fiction *The Clothing of Books* (2017), she has mentioned the hiatus between the author and the designer and such covering of the book has nicely been compared to translation also:

> The more I think about it, the more I am convinced that a cover is a sort of translation, that is, an interpretation of my words into another language — a visual one. It represents the text, but it isn't part of it. It can't be too literal. It has to have its own take on the book. Like a translation, a cover can be faithful to the book, or it can be misleading. In theory, like a translation, it should be in the service of the book, but this dynamic isn't always the case. A cover can be overbearing, dominating. Whatever the outcome, a cover imposes an intimate relationship between author and image. This is why it can lead to a sense of complete alienation. (*The Clothing of Books* 17-18)

Hence, as in her essay "*Intimate Alienation*: Immigrant Fiction and Translation" she has expressed 'I translate therefore I am'(5) which is referring to her departure from any particular location via continuous translation of her own and celebrating her intimacy with alienation; such impact can be resonated in her latest published work *The Clothing of Books* where covering of the book is compared to the translation, and such imposition of intimate relationship between the author and image, which book cover unfurls, is inevitably leading towards absolute alienation. In fact, under the garb of production house while the books are being released, it seems to refer to consumerism or commodity fetishism, which caters to the demands of public, not the demands of the author; it results in intimate alienation of the author Jhumpa Lahiri. In fine, alienation is a stage of dissatisfaction, dissociation and rejection in terms of divergence between what is real and what is utopian or ideal. In fact, an alienated individual is dissatisfied, inimical to the dominant concerns, values, norms and activities of the society and s/he can be alienated from himself or herself in the familial space, too, which results in individual's feeling of anxiety, despair, anger, loneliness, emptiness, purposelessness, loss of identity, resentment, disgust and sadness. However, such journey of a diasporic individual like the author Jhumpa Lahiri and her works are also testifying to such alienation and continuous possibility, too, being a cultural translator. Lahiri unveils the similar tune in *Whereabouts* (2021) through the portrayal of an unnamed female narrator, an attractive middle-aged academic living in Italy, attempts to seek salvation in her Italian syntax. The unnamed narrator's account helps one see how Lahiri enters into the role of the interpreter of families' 'private morphologies'. The narrator is a woman of a different mould, who is to some extent different from the usual Lahirivian women characters depicted in her earlier works. She seems to show Jhumpa Lahiri the path toward herself off the extreme solipsism as manifested in *In Other Words*. The narrator minutely observes her own different selves: that of a single woman. She is addicted to solitude, but not averse to having affairs. She is a tired teacher, a terrible daughter, a solicitous friend, a survivor. Moreover, it is a story of the collective condition of the in-between people inhabiting the changing world where identity, being, and belonging are in a constant state of oscillation. She says, "Is there any place we are not moving through" (*Whereabouts* 153). She is fond of movement, instability and temporality. She enjoys her hybrid identity which she feels enriched. Hence, she states,

> On the one hand I want desperately to belong, to have a clear identity. On the other, I refuse to belong, and I believe that my hybrid identity enriches me. I will probably always remain torn between these two roads, these two impulses. (*The Clothing of Books* 64)

Lahiri after *The Lowland*, starts demonstrating her different journey into Italianness. Despite Being an established writer in a strong language, she takes challenge to begin her journey anew by resorting to Italian language and seeks to be accepted. She competently develops her personality through her arduous linguistic as well as cultural journey. She brings out the contradictions, possible dichotomies between East and west, her unfulfilled desire, and her loss and gain. Lahiri reveals how to admire differences and how to invent the newness in people as well as situations. She indicates boundary crossing as a defense against particularisms and nationalisms. Lahiri's new place and new languages have given her a new vision to look at the world differently and thus she represents her literary transition. The *Italian phase* which she has adopted at present propels the readers to delve deep into the Lahirivian works in order to identify her literary stature; it is absolutely aporetic and so is replate with her inherent instability like that of a signifier and a signified in a sign system, connoting her literary transgression.

Bibliography

Primary Sources:

Lahiri, Jhumpa. *Interpreter of Maladies: Stories of Bengal, Boston, and Beyond*. New Delhi: Harper Collins India, 1999. Rpt. 2000.

—."Intimate Alienation: Immigrant Fiction and Translation" (2002).*University of Macerata E-Documents*. Accessed on 1 January 2017 <*http://docenti.un imc.it/sharifah.alatas/teaching/2015/2000004111/files/lm37-ii-anno-first-sem ester/Intimate%20Alienation.doc/at_download/file*>

—. *The Namesake*. New York: Houghton Mifflin Company, 2003.

—. "The Long Way Home: Bengal by Way of Julia Child". *The New Yorker* 6 September 2004: 83.

—. "My Two Lives". *Newsweek* 6 March 2006: 43.

—. *Unaccustomed Earth*. New York: Houghton Mifflin Company, 2008.

—. *The Lowland*. Noida: Random House Publishers India, 2013.

—. *The Clothing of Books*. New York: Vintage Books, 2015.

—. *In Other Words*. Trans. Ann Goldstein. New York: Knopf, 2016.

—. *The Penguine Book of Italian Short Stories*. Ed. Jhumpa Lahiri. Italy: Penguine Random House, 2019.

—. *Whereabouts*. Trans. Jhumpa Lahiri. India: Penguin,2021.

—.*Translating Myself and Others*. Trans. Jhumpa Lahiri. Princeton University Press, 2022.

Secondary Sources:

Ahmed, Sara. *The Cultural Politics of Emotion*. New York: Routledge, 2004.

Aikant, Satish C. "Culture and Resistance in the Indian English Novel". *Nation in Imagination*. Ed. C Vijayasree, Mennakshi Mukherjee, Harish Trivedi, and T Vijay Kumar. New Delhi: Orient Blackswan, 2012. 58-71.

Anderson, Benedict. *Imagined Communities: Reflections on the origin and spread of Nationalism*. London: Verso, 1983.

Appadurai, Arjun. *Modernity at Large: Cultural Dimensions of Globalization*. New Delhi: Oxford University Press India, 1997.

Aristotle. *Politics*. Trans. Carnes Lord. Chicago: The University of Chicago Press, 2013.

Ashcroft, Bill. "Postcolonial Horizons". *(In)Fusion Approach: Theory, Contestation, Limits: (In)fusioning a few Indian English Novels.* Ed. Ranjan Ghosh. New York: Oxford Universty Press U.S.A., 2006.

—."Globalization, the Transnation, and Utopia". *Narrating The (Trans)Nation: The Dialectics of Culture and Identity.* Eds. Krishna Sen, and Sudeshna Chakravarty. Kolkata: Das Gupta & Co. Pvt. Ltd., 2008. 1-24.

—. "Transcultural Presence". *Storia della Striografia* 55 (2009): 76-93.

Bakhtin, Mikhail, Mikhailo Vinch, and Mihael Holquist. *The Dialogical Imagination: Four Essays.* Austin: University of Texas Press, 1981.

Benhabib, Seyla. *Another Cosmopolitanism.* Ed. Robert Post. New York: Oxford University Press U.S.A., 2006.

Bhabha, Homi. *The Location of Culture.* New York: Routledge, 2004.

Biswas, MunMun Das. "Jhumpa Lahiri's interview with Elizabeth Fransworth— *Theme of Displacement and Loneliness: A Study of Jhumpa Lahiri's Interpreter of Maladies*" P.I.J.M.S. 1.1 (2014): 81-82.

Brah, Avtar. *Cartographies of Diaspora: Contesting Identities.* New York: Routledge, 2005.

Caruth, Cathy. *Unclaimed Experience.* Baltimore: John Hopkins University Press, 1996.

Chatterjee, Partha. *The Nation and Its Fragments: Colonial and Postcolonial Histories.* Princeton: Princeton University Press, 1993.

Cheah, Pheng. *Spectral Nationality: Passages of Freedom from Kant to Postcolonial Literature of Liberation.* New York: Columbia University Press, 2003.

Choate, Mark I. *Emigrant Nation: The Making Of Italy Abroad.* London: Harvard University Press, 2008.

Clifford, J. *The Predicament of Culture.* Cambridge: Harvard University Press, 1988.

Derrida, Jacques. 'Living on/Border Lines'. *Deconstruction and Criticism.* Trans. James Hulbert. Ed. Harold Bloom. London: Continuum, 2004.

Devy. Ganesh. *Cultural Amnesia. Shodhganga.* Accessed on 6 August 2018. Available at: *http://.Shodhganga.inflibnet.ac.in/bitstream/10603/4107/9/0 9_chapter%204,pdf.*

Dhingra, Lavina, and Floyd Cheung (eds). *Naming Jhumpa Lahiri: Canons and Controversies.* Lanham: Lexington Books, 2012.

Eliot, T.S. "Little Gidding", in Eliot, *Four Quartets* (1943; Orlando Fl: Harcourt, 1971): 49-59.

Fanon, Franz. *The Wretched of the Earth.* Trans. Richard Philcox. New York: Grove Press, 2004.

Foucault, Michel. *Madness and Civilization: A History of Insanity in the age of Reason.* Trans. Richard Howard. London and New York: Routledge, 2001.

Freud, Sigmund. "Mourning and Melancholia". *The Standard Edition of the Complete Psychological Works of Sigmund Freud.* London: Hogarth, 1955: 243.

Ghoshal, Somak. "The Lives of Others". LiveMint. 25 January 2014. Accessed on 5 July 2017. <http://www.livemint.com/Leisure/zWhN5FKCyq3Mci96bD7nWO/Jhumpa-Lahiri--The-Lives-of-others.html

Gikandi, Simon."Globalization and the Claims of Postcoloniality". *Postcolonialisms: An Anthology of Cultural Theory and Criticism.* Ed.Gaurav Desai and Supriya Nair. Oxford: Berg, 2005.

Gilroy, Paul. *The Black Atlantic: Modernity and Double Consciousness.* New York: Verso, 2002.

Heidegger, Martin. *Being and Time.* Trans. Joan Stambaugh. Albany: New York Press, 2010.

Hirsch, Marianne. "Past Lives:Postmemories in Exile", Poetics Today, Vol.17, No.4 (Winter 1996): 662.

Hooks, Bell. *"Eating the Other*: Desire and Resistance". *The Consumer Society Reader.* Eds. Juliet B. Schor, and Douglas B. Holt. New York: New York Press, 2000: 343-69.

Huddart, David. *Homi K Bhabha.* London and NewYork: Routledge, 2006.

Iskandar, Adel and Hakem Rustom (eds). *Edward Said: A Legacy of Emancipation and Representation.* London: University of California Press, 2010

Kant, Immanuel. *Perpetual Peace.* New York: Cosmico, 2010.

Keuler, Andrew. "Pulitzer-Winning author, BU alum speaks about new book". The Daily Free Press. 20 February 2014. Accessed on 12 July 2017. http://dailyfreepress.com/2014/02/20/Pulitzer-winning-author-and-alum-speaks-to-bu-about-new-book.

Kierkegaard, Søren. *The Sickness unto Death.* Trans. Howard V. Hong and Edna H. Hong. Princeton: Princeton University Press, 1980.

Kivisto, Peter. *Multiculturalism in a Global Society.* Oxford: Blackwell Publishers, 2002.

Klages, Mary. *Literary Theory: A Guide For the Perplexed.* New York: Continuum, 2008.

Kraniauskas, John."Hybridity in a transnational frame: Latin-Americanist and Post-Colonial Perspectives on Cultural Studies". *Hybridity and its Discontents: Politics, Science, Culture.* Eds. Avtar Brah, and Annie E. Coombes. London and New York: Routledge, 2000. 235-256.

Krips, Henry. *Fetish: An Erotics of Culture.* New York: Cornell University Press, 1999.

Lahiri, Himadri. "Individual-Family Interface in Jhumpa Lahiri's *The Namesake*". *Americana* 4.2 (2008): n.Pag.Web. 13 May 2015.

—."Jhumpa Lahiri's *The Namesake*: Identity and Representation". *Contemporary Perspectives on English Studies.* Eds. Chandana John Chatterjee, T. Diana Jecob, Vangeepnram Sreenatha Chary and T.D. Peter. New Delhi: Creative Publisher, 2018. 131-153.

Lee, Brain. *Theory and Personality: The Significance of T.S. Eliot's Criticism.* London: Bloomsbury Publishing, 2013.

Levi-Strauss, Claude. *Structural Anthropology.* Trans. Claire Jacobson and Brooke Schoepf. New York: Basic Books,1963.

Llewellyn, John. *The Hypocritical Imagination: Between Kant and Levinas.* New York: Routledge, 2000.

Lyotard, Jean-Francois. *The Postmodern Condition: A Report on Knowledge*: Minneapolis: University of Minnesota Press, 1984.

Mandal, Somdatta. *Asian-American Writing: The Diasporic Imagination.* Vol 3. New Delhi; Prestige Books, 2000

Mannur, Anita. *Culinary Fictions: Food in South-Asian Diasporic Culture.* Philadelphia: Temple University Press, 2010.

Matravers, Matt. *Managing Modernity: Politics and the Culture of Control.* New York: Routledge, 2005.

Mishra, Sudesh. "*From Sugar to Masala*: Writings by the Indian Diaspora." *An Illustrated History of Indian Literature in English.* Ed. A.K. Malhotra. New Delhi: Permanent Black, 2003. 276-94.

Mishra, Vijay. *The Literature of the Indian Diaspora: Theorising the Diasporic Imaginary.* London: Routledge, 2007.

Mogford, Sheilagha. "The Murder of the Goddess in Everywoman: Mary Daly's Sado-Ritual Syndrome and Margaret Atwood's *The Handmaid's Tale*". *Feminist Interpretations of Mary Daly.* Eds. Sarah Lucia Hoagland and Marilyn Frye. Pennsylvania: The Pennsylvania State University Press, 2000. 136-37.

Munos, Delphine. *After Melancholia: A Reappraisal of Second-Generation Diasporic Subjectivity in the work of Jhumpa Lahiri.* New York: Rodopi, 2013.

Osborn, John. *Look Back in Anger.* London: Penguin, 1957.

Roudinesco, Elizabeth. *Jacques Lacan & Co: A History of Psychoanalysis in France, 1925-1985.* Trans. Jeffrey Mehlman. Chicago: The University of Chicago Press, 1990.

Rushdie, Salman. *Imaginary Homelands.* London: Vintage Books, 2010.

Safran, William. "Diasporas in Modern Societies: Myths of Homeland and Return". *Diaspora: A Journal of Transnational Studies*. 1.1 (1991):83.

Said, Edward W. *The Mind of Winter: Reflections on life in exile 1984*. New York: Harper, 1984.

Scarry, Elaine. *The Body in Pain*. New York: Oxford University Press U.S.A., 1985.

Schroeder, Severin. *Wittgenstein: The Way out of the Fly-Bottle*. Cambridge: Polity Press, 2006.

Sen, Amartya. *Identity and Violence: The Illusion of Destiny*. London: Penguin, 2003.

Seymour, Laura. *Roland Barthes's The Death of the Author*. New York: Taylor & Francis, 2018.

Shankar, Lavinia D. "Not Too Spicy: Exotic Mistresses of Cultural Translation in the Fiction of Chitra Divakaruni and Jhumpa Lahiri". *Other Tongues: Rethinking the Language Debate in India*. Eds. Nalini Iyer, and Bonnie Zare. Amsterdam: Rodopi, 2009. 41.

Soja, Edward W. *Postmodern Geographies: The Re-assertion of Space in Critical Social Theory*. London: Verso, 1989.

—.*Third Space: Journeys to Los Angeles and Other Real-and-Imagined Places*. Hoboken: Blackwell Publishers, 2000.

Spivak, Gayatri. "Can the Subaltern Speak?" *Colonial Discourse and Postcolonial Theory: A Reader*. Ed. Patrick Williams and Laura Chrisman. New York: Columbia University Press, 1994.

Trivedi, Harish. "Translating Culture vs Cultural Translation". *91st Meridian* 4.1 (Spring 2005):1-8.

Tagore, Rabindranath. *Nationalism*. New York: Macmillan, 1918.

Vertovec, Steven. *The Hindu Diaspora*. London: Routledge, 2000.

Vitale, Tom."Transplanted Author Finds Roots in Writing". *N.P.R.*8 September 2008. Accessed on 7 October 2018 https://www.npr.org/templates/story/story.php!StoryId=89311782

Williams, Raymond. *Culture and Society*. New York: Columbia University Press, 1983.

Yegenoglu, Sertan. *Colonial Fantasies: Towards Feminist Reading of Orientalism*. Cambridge: Cambridge University Press, 1998.

Young, Robert J.C. *Colonial Desire: Hybridityin Theory, Culture, and Race*. London and New York: Routledge, 2003.

Index

ABCD 23, 29, 134

Absolute Other 35, 37, 39

Adler, Alfred 93

Agamben, Georgio 4, 6

Ahmed, Sara 40, 48

Alienation 10, 15, 16, 20, 23, 24, 25, 27, 28, 29, 30, 33, 34, 35, 39, 41, 46, 48, 50, 52, 54, 56, 57, 60, 63, 67, 71, 72, 76, 77, 80, 98, 102, 103, 113, 118, 129, 130, 131, 132, 133, 135, 136, 137

Amateur 122

Ambiguity 30, 128

Ambivalence 10, 29, 109, 127

Amnesia 51, 52

Anamnesis 28

Anderson, Benedict 16, 20

Another Cosmopolitanism 19

Aporia 86

Appadurai, Arjun 11, 16, 24

Aristotle 46

Ashcroft, Bill 20

Asian American masculinity 101

Bakhtin, Mikhail 29, 104

Barel ife 46, 47, 132

Barthes, Roland 60

Behdad, Ali 22

Benhabib, Seyla 19

Benjamin, Walter 129

Bhabha, Homi 95, 129

Bhat, Gauri 24, 87

Blunt, Alison 62

Brah, Avtar 16, 96

Brain drain 15

Broken mirror 107

Browning, Robert 115

Cartographical epistemology 29, 50, 96, 107, 129, 134

Caruth, Cathy 26

Catachresis 85, 134

Chatterjee, Partha 82

Choate, Mark 111, 112

Chronotopes 29, 106, 135

Chutnification 20

Culinary citizenship 134

Cyber Coolies 15

Daly, Mary 5, 3, 54, 132

Deleuze, Gilles 17

Democratic iteration 19

Derrida, Jacques 98, 129

Devy, G.N 51, 52

Dhingra, Lavina 26, 43, 84, 93

Dialectic 5, 9, 27, 35, 39, 50, 51, 57, 86, 94, 95, 120, 133, 134

Dialogic connection 25, 28, 42

Diaspora 9, 14, 15, 16, 18, 23, 25, 27, 28, 31, 48, 53, 56, 57, 73, 81, 86, 92, 96, 106, 129

Diasporic Public sphere 16

Diasporic subjectivity 5, 16, 20, 130, 131

Difference 15, 19, 31, 33, 34, 35, 40, 46, 52, 57, 64, 67, 74, 81, 83, 86, 88, 94, 95, 115, 134, 138

Disinterestedness 100, 110, 123

Dissident voices 20

Divakaruni, Chitra Banerjee 14, 21, 100

Double Consciousness 18

Eliot, T.S. 13, 50, 51, 52

Ethnicity 24

Ethnoscapes 33

Family 81, 112

Fanon, Frantz 48

Forever Foreigner 93

Foucault, Michel 46, 82

Fractured perception 107

Frost, Robert 18

Ghettoization 13, 62

Gikandi, Simon 99, 130

Gilroy, Paul 71

Global Capitalism 15

Global flow 92, 99, 130

Global transnationalism 68

Glocal 15, 18

Governmentaliy 82

Habitus 31

Hawthorne 59

Hegel 19, 34, 35

Heidegger, Martin 116

Hirsch, Mariam 75

Homelessness 15, 27

Homing Desire 63, 64, 83

Hooks, Bell 49, 50, 131

Husserl, Edmund 95, 96

Hybridity 26, 30, 106, 134

Hypen 15

Imagination 16, 17, 19, 23, 40, 61, 64, 72, 83, 98, 104, 120, 127

Imagined Community 16, 22

In-betweenness 29, 81

Inherent Instability 20, 138

Intimate space 28, 39, 42, 131

Intimate alienation 23, 24, 25, 30, 52, 71, 72, 118, 130, 132, 133, 135, 136

Italian language 13, 19, 27, 30, 109, 110, 111, 112, 113, 114, 115, 116, 117, 118, 119, 120, 121, 123, 124, 125, 126, 127, 135, 137

Italian phase 5, 28, 29, 30, 109, 127, 128, 135, 138

Jouissance 115

Kant, Immanuel 23, 117, 130

Kivisto, Peter 129

Klages, Marry 102

Lefebvre, Henry 40

Levinas 67

Liminality 130

Linguistic dislocation 10, 13, 30

Linguistic hegemony 124

Loss 5, 15, 26, 27, 29, 30, 33, 34, 38, 43, 44, 45, 48, 56, 60, 63, 72, 74, 75, 76, 77, 82, 83, 93, 96, 97, 106, 122, 128, 131, 132, 134, 137, 138

Lyotard, Jean Francois 130

Maladies 5, 13, 26, 28, 33, 34, 36, 42, 57, 101, 106, 131

Mannur, Anita 90

Masala diaspora 15

Memory 17, 24, 28, 39, 41, 43, 45, 46, 6 2, 68, 75, 78, 83, 92, 99, 101, 105, 107, 132, 133

Micro-narratives 20

Milles, Sarah 19

Mishra, Sudesh 53

Mishra, Vijay 4, 4, 116

Model minority 15, 17, 55, 56, 87

Motherhood 100

Munos, Delphine 26, 73, 75, 76, 78, 133

Nationalism 11, 18, 19, 28, 40, 57, 83, 99, 112, 138

Naxalite movement 29, 96, 97, 98, 99, 101, 103, 107, 127, 134

Neo-Indian womanhood 102, 107

Nietzsche 35, 132

Oedipal tension 77, 133

Osborne, John 38

Panopticon 47

Partition 48, 131

Polyphonic voices 131

Postcards 61, 62, 113, 133

Postcolonial horizontality 98

Postmemory 75, 133

Post-nostalgic phase 92

Rushdie, Salman 20, 27, 33, 107, 132

Safran, William 16, 116

Same-sex affair 29, 101, 102, 135

Scarry, Elain 43

Sen, Amartya 129

Skempton 34

Softspace 15

Sovereignty 47

Spectralization 98

Spivak, Gayatri 27, 85, 134

Strauss, Levis 44, 45

Suturing 20, 120

Tagore, Rabindranath 18, 55, 100

Third language 93

Thrownness 116

Transcultural encounter 20, 96, 131

Transgenerational phantoms 133

Transgression 11, 28, 47, 54, 56,
    130, 138

Translation 11, 14, 25, 26, 27, 30,
    118, 121, 124, 129, 130, 132,
    135, 136

Translocation 1, 5

Transmigrants 129

Transnationalism   2, 8, 68, 81,
    129, 131

Transplantation 60

Trauma 20, 26, 29, 43, 44, 45, 75,
    92

Trivedi, Harish 26, 118, 124

Uncanny space 20, 101

Unconditional hospitality 19, 59

Untranslatibility   28, 45, 124,
    129, 130

Vaccum Culture 24, 87

Walker, Alice 102

Will to power 54, 132

William, Reymond 95

Wittgenstein 111

Yeats, W.B. 20

Young, Robert J.C 14, 17

Auritra Munshi's book is an important addition to the critical examination of the well-known South Asian diasporic writer Jhumpa Lahiri. He efficiently demonstrates how Lahiri is to be now considered as more than a diasporic writer – but rather a transnational global voice.
—Prof. Mala Pandurang, Professor of English and Principal, Dr BMN College, SNDT Women's University, Mumbai, India.

This book provides a comprehensive overview of Jhumpa Lahiri's entire oeuvre.
—Himadri Lahiri, Professor Emeritus, Department of English and Culture Studies, The University of Burdwan, West Bengal, India

What is particularly interesting is the attention Auritra Munshi pays to Lahiri's later works, especially those belonging to what may be called her 'Italian phase'. His book will be a great value addition to anyone interested in Jhumpa Lahiri's writings and the very many questions of contemporary concern she raises and is interested in. A pleasure to read.
—Prof. Simi Malhotra, Professor & Head, Department of English, Director, Centre for Innovation and Entrepreneurship, Jamia Millia Islamia (A Central University), New Delhi, India.

An invaluable contribution to scholarship on Jhumpa Lahiri.
—Prof. Amrit Sen, Professor, Department of English and Other Modern European Languages (DEOMEL), Visva-Bharati, Santiniketan, India